To my favorite auntie,

MW01705880

s.

Love, Heather Rose
XO

Routes

Twelve poets.
A road less traveled.

BeWrite Books, UK
www.bewrite.net

Published internationally by BeWrite Books, UK.
32 Bryn Road South, Wigan, Lancashire, WN4 8QR.

British Library Cataloguing in Publication Data. A catalogue record for this book is available from the British Library

ISBN 1-904492-60-6

Also available in eBook format from www.bewrite.net

Digitally produced by BeWrite Books

Cover image: Heather Grace Stewart © 2004

Acknowledgements

Carillon Magazine, The Peoples Poet, Panda and Aesthetica.

Contents

John Thomson

Clive Warner

Kathryn McL Collins

Dazz Jackson

Tom O Campbell

Heather Grace Stewart

John G Hall

Heather Bryant

Introduction

They are test drivers, filmmakers, cooks, editors, soldiers, lawyers, photographers, radio station installers, from Mexico, Quebec, Portugal, the eastern United States, the American south, Wales and more.

And they share within these pages a love of words, of technique, of expression, of experimentation.

Yet for the majority of these poets, writing is not a paying career. Going through the routines of life, they steal a moment from a busy wage-earning day to record a feeling, a scene, an event … then return to the mundane.

Such is the life of the modern day poet, with car payments, lawns to mow, wars to worry about, and children to chase after.

Poetry is an incredibly hard field in which to maintain faith. But the poets in this book stuck to their routes and have continued to write; some for a year, some for twenty years, with no hope or desire for fame, far less fortune.

Through the centuries, the art of poetry has been about the wonder of human expression, the beauty of clear communication. Unlike some other forms of writing, it has never been valued in terms of dollars and cents. Poets do not write for financial gain. Payment is the invitation to allow poets the weaving of their unique spell.

I'm grateful for the opportunity to have worked with each and every one of these generous gift-makers, and awed by the responsibility entrusted to me to compile a collection of their most treasured words.

I am honored that these selfless wordsmiths gathered together in the non-commercial environment of BeWrite.net – the huge, warm community of international creative talent in which I play my part – with no more desired return than the stirring in the reader's soul.

This collection is compiled with thanks to its fine contributors, fellow poet and editorial colleague Heather Grace Stewart, our publishers, BeWrite Books, who provide a platform where others might not.

And to readers everywhere who understand that a ploughman can write of mice and men and a king of green sleeves.

Heather Bryant

Routes

Andrew Proudfoot

my life in parenthesis

when i am old
(older than i am now)
i will always be first in the queue
(whether or not i *am* first in the queue)

and i will take the best seat
(your seat)
in the park
(and on the bus)

you will visit
(every other sunday)
with your children
(my grandchildren)

a fortnightly ritual
on the periphery of your lives

and i will remember the war
(frequently)
and childhood
(in detail)
and yesterday
(as if it had never happened)

yes, when i am old
(older than i am now)
i will live my life in parentheses
(yours)

(and mine)

later, the table

at first
it was the little things
that went unnoticed

a week ago last Tuesday
the salt cellar and the garlic press
snuck off together
keenly followed
by the bread knife and the cutlery

encouraged
by this mini Great Escape,
yet with furtive glances,
larger items
took their chances

the bedside lamp
(under cover of darkness)
came out of the shade
and,
unhappy with the way things are,
departed with the VCR

later, the table,
furnished with lame excuses
and with the chairs acting as decoy,
turned, and slipped away

this isn't how
it's meant to be
my home is slowly
leaving me

cry

it’s all right to cry
if you’re lonely,
we all do, now and then.
and you can cry
if you’re scared.
we all get scared.
and you can cry if it hurts
whatever it is
it’s all right.

but
if you hear them coming,
and you’re lonely
and scared
and it hurts, whatever it is,
cry quietly.

the wishing tree

it was ten years later
and we lay
after love
and in love

shall we go back
to the wishing tree
you said
and we drove
half the day

and found the track
at the foot of the hill
a sign, now by the fence,
read simply: *to the tree*

we half walked
half ran
passing others
coming and going
all smiling

until we reached the tree
our tree
the wishing tree

and everywhere we looked
small scraps of paper
an autumn blossom
tied to the lower branches
with hope
and coloured thread

ours, the first,
long gone of course

you turned
and mouthed
a silent kiss

we both remembered
our first wish
that others could be
like us, like this

in a little place

before this
i lived in a big place

with loads of space
for others
to invade
and make themselves comfortable
and leave

now
i live in a little place

it's me-sized
you see
so you can't get in

and Deidre smiled

bag in hand
and
hand on heart
(my chest proclaiming
jesus would smoke pot)
i passed through the green channel

Deidre
(if her name-badge was to be believed)
beckoned.
She took,
and opened for a second,
my passport

"occupation poet?"
"yes," i said
"what's in the bag?"
"words," i said
"and did you pack it all alone?"
i nodded
"yes, they're all my own"

Deidre opened the bag,
and took out words at random.

in addition to my smalls
(the little words)
she found
(hiding amongst *love, dreams* and *beautiful sunsets*)
drugs and *handguns*

"i can explain," i said
"look!"
and pointed
at the words she had placed
on the counter:

in the Autumn
many drugs distracted her
and fragments of beautiful sunsets
were but handguns to the mind

under one universe
or another
she dreams

he was Infinity
she was Love,
always

"very good"
i said

and Deidre,
lost for words,
smiled

Ptolemy 1, Rest of the World 0

the earth is flat
and rests
on a turtle's back

the earth is not flat
and does not rest

Lemon Chewing

I

you'll forget your head
one of these days,
you said

and one of those days i did…

i must wear my cap in school
i must wear my cap in school
i must wear my cap in school
i must wear my cap in school…

II

you'll be for the high jump
if you do that again,
you said

so i practiced well
and i did it again…

i'll come down soon
i'll come down soon,
i'm fosbury flopping
over the moon

III

you'll stay like that
if the wind changes,
you said

and one still day,
caught unawares
chewing a lemon…

i felt a breeze
i felt a breeze
i felt a breeze

throwing stones

what i like about this place
is the glassless windows

what i like about glassless windows
is the music
especially the violins

and the walls,
within which

what i like about glassless windows
is the wildlife,
and the kindness of others

and the walls,
in spite of which

what i like about glassless windows
is the leaves,
the silence in between

and the walls,
without which

but what i like most
about glassless windows
is the way the world comes in
and the opportunities for stone throwing

Art in Heaven

Dear Santa,

First, a thank-you
for recent gifts.
The Spandau Ballet CD
and the horror video
have been much appreciated.
Perhaps something more enigmatic this time?

Love, Jesus

ps: my Father loved the painting set last year

Dear Jesus,

Thank-you for your letter.
So glad you enjoyed Gold
and Frankenstein.
Will ask Mrs Claus and the elves
to come up with a real surprise this year.

Love, Santa

ps: can't wait to see your Father's art in Heaven

please look after this poem

I found this poem
on the bus
on the vacant seat
the beautiful stranger having gone

And I found this poem
in Starbucks
at the empty table

I found this poem
wide awake
at three in the morning

And I found this poem
half asleep
daydreaming
in the middle of the afternoon

I found this poem
difficult
like a teenager

And I found this poem
tender
and afraid

I found this poem
full of hope
and the most fragilest
(like *hope* and *fragilest*)

please look after this poem

Ten Ways to Wear Snow

1. Majestically. Like mountains. Cathedrals.

2. Softly, gently. Fresh sheets. A new lover.

3. Playfully. Like angels' wings. A snowball, mid-flight.

4. Heartachingly beautifully. Your face.

5. Festively. The morning after the Christmas Eve before.

6. Dramatically. Like an avalanche. A village. A small hand.

7. Like guilt. Whitewash. A clean slate.

8. Quietly. Like a whisper, a blessing. A shroud in waiting.

9. Silently.

10.

room for manoeuvre

history,
it seems to me,
(not normally one of the creative arts)
nevertheless
has some room for manoeuvre

what if
dinosaurs were microscopic,
Jesus was nocturnal,
if Hitler always dressed in pink,
his underpants external

would Bonnie or Clyde
have worked as well
alone?
would John of Arc
have burned
as well as Joan?

Would Now
Be here,
    or here,
        or here?

If yesterday were different
today, would anything seem possible?

ever so close

was it ever so close,
the future?

the child's hand
in the drowning lake.

the siren's wail
in the last heartbeat
of the car crash.

as close as the rocks
in the mind
of Lovers' Leap

as close as the telling
in the secrets
that we keep

was it ever so close?

and was it ever so far away?

My spacebar is oblivious

my cheese plant has reneged
on our unspoken agreement
and spectacularly failed
to bear
any form of dairy product

likewise
the monkey-puzzle tree
has produced
neither monkeys
nor puzzles

(the wardrobe, thankfully,
is at peace)

and my spacebar too,
despite
evidencetothecontrary,
fails to recognise
the distance between meandyou

Jan Oskar Hansen

The Sadness of Sex

"Look, I've lost weight, my legs are slimmer
don't you think?" "They look lovely," I say,
pat her generous behind, try to avoid looking
at legs full of rivers and lakes, and for no reason
at all I think of Finland. "You haven't been
kind to me lately, are you avoiding me?" she
says, and coyly wriggles her sixty-year-old
body. A glass of brandy would be
handy now that I've got to do my duty – I want
to avoid being a lonely old man.

Her Garden

Late afternoon in her garden, surrounded by
exotic flowers that exude the heavy perfume
of longings with no name. The battered
back door, once green, now cracked white,
is ajar. She comes out, her face is drawn and
too-early aged. The faint smell of alcohol
lingers on her breath. I put my arm
around her, but am distressed by her
eternal loneliness. I have no love to
give her.

Bomb Storms

When the siren wailed
and fingers of light clawed
at the cold night sky,
mother put her winter coat on,
wrapped me in a blanket,
and ran to the bomb shelter
in the basement of a school –
the only building not made of timber.
The school shook several times; faces
froze to statues in my mind.
When we came out, a nearby factory
was ablaze; hot debris thawed
an icy road.
Nightly alarms became routine,
but mother never again
took us to that bomb shelter.
She didn't like the idea of the school
collapsing on top of us. Instead, she always
unhooked the glass-pearl ceiling lamp. It
absorbed our flickering
candlelight, returning it
as tiny rainbows.

If Only

In a flat winter landscape, a lone tree wrote
on a blackboard sky. For chalk it used a fallen star.
I'm alone, rooted to frozen soil, can't fly like
the sparrows that use me as a resting place,
fly away when blue. Today I wish to be a tree
in a forest: entwine my roots with a lady tree,
strew my auburn harvest and protect a grateful
ground. Failing that, I wish to be a palm tree on
a tropical island, where my branches protect
wild goats from rain. Only in winters though,
in spring I want to be myself: a green-leafed tree
that makes a flat landscape less bleak.

The Raven

If I see a hundred ravenous jet-black ravens
in a field feasting on a pregnant dead sheep,
should I accept it as a fact that all ravens
are barbarians, or should I go on looking till
I find an angelic white one, which doesn't
feed on dead things, but daintily eats berries
in a shimmering Nordic twilight? And if its
snowy plumage has spots of red beneath its
lemon yellow beak, should I assume that it's
strawberry juice, not a sparrow's
blood? A white raven could not possibly do
harm to anyone smaller than itself.

Calcutta

My ship docked there once. I went ashore and ended up on
the wrong side of the railway track. Walked through streets in
a trance due to heat, colours the stench of poverty and booze
sold at illicit places. Tried not to step on prone humanity and, dodging
beggars, came upon a dying hospital; a send-off dock
for the poor. Skeletal men and women on straw mats, being prepared for
the long voyage on the ocean of forever by haloed nuns in blue
uniforms. An old woman, almost transparent, held out her hand and said
in Hindi, a language I don't understand but did that night: "Oh, there
you are, what took you so long?" Knelt by her side, took her hand, a
fluttering sparrow in my palm. "I've been travelling the world trying
to find a spiritual homeland. Tell me about your journey."
I did, told her about my endless grief, the lost home and those I loved.
The beauty of sunsets and sunrises over a glorious ocean. The sparrow
wings fluttered no more, mother smiled; her voyage across the sea of
serenity had begun. A nun touched my shoulder and I walked out into the
brutal heat of Calcutta. My sorrow had been consoled
and the burden of guilt lifted.

Frederica

At the home for abandoned dogs, I was caught in the radar
of her brown eyes – love at first sight – and the clamour of
other more subservient dogs ceased. Tan and white, legs too
short: a middle aged, spayed spinster, but she's got style and
a supreme contempt for other dogs. Back home I fed her
a tin of dog food left in the fridge since my other dog died;
she jumped up on the sofa, I chased her off: our first argument.
Wakes me up at seven by jumping on the bed and licking my face. I hate
that, but the lady needs to go outside and do her thing. If she thinks
I have been too long indoors she pesters me till I grumpily relent
and take her for a walk. We are set in our ways, can't teach each other
new tricks, and every morning there is dog hair on the sofa.

A Childhood

A sink bucket hung on a nail on the flaking kitchen
wall and, wrapped around it, a blue towel. In the mornings
we washed our faces under a cold water tap and, since
there were four of us, each one had a corner of the towel.
On Saturdays the bucket was taken down, placed on
a stool, filled with hot water;
naked feet on yesterday's paper
to protect the lino, and thus we strip-washed
from head to foot but were left with newsprint on our
socks-darned-a-thousand-times, but rich we were; we had
shelves full of books that could take us on journeys to
foreign shores, and back in time for the children's hour
on the radio.

Buenos Aires 1978

The evening approached as day's vanishing light slinked
its way across the pampas, night came and filled the town
with a distinctive smell of food, lust and random violence.
In a bar a man sat picking pieces of glass off his face while
drinking cold beer, the barkeeper laid on the floor, his third
eye glinted in coloured lights; covered his face with a napkin
on which a red rose sprung, helped myself to a brandy.
When police sirens grew louder I blended with shadows outside,
such a drag to be asked questions I couldn't answer.
The night was still young and desire for life drove me to visit
a cathouse. Danced tangos with a woman whose tits rested
on my shoulders, hypnotized by her unblinking wicked eyes
and enormous lips which hovered over my head;
saliva dripped till dawn came creeping back from the pampas.

The Drinker

There is a general assumption, in our increasingly
pleasure-less time, that those who drink must be
an unhappy lot. I know of a woman who sups so
much that her liver sometimes gasps for air, but
she enjoys every drop of her wine. Her world is
a contented one, as seen through a glass of golden
liquid, she drinks her sun and thus avoids getting
wrinkled skin. She's happy in her own reality and
I shudder to think what would happen if the do-gooders
ever got hold of her and showed her their
reality through brutally-polished spectacles.

Days of Silence

My village is so quiet that I can hear flies talk. Mostly they chatter about food, enormous predatory sparrows and wars they wage against bees. A fly wrote a book on the surface of my coffee table, thousands came and read before the cleaner, with her yellow duster, arrived. The book's sagacity became part of dipterans' collective memories. Aware of their own worth they no longer buzz softly in corners, turn their noses up when offered cow dung; only a beer drinker's vomit, rancid butter and horse manure will suffice. Oh dipterous, confident insect, do whatever you like, but don't crawl up a mule's nose, wash your face in an open latrine and then leave tiny pellets of excreta in the sugar bowl.

a song for a housewife

Oh wide-hipped, heavy-bosomed housewife, carrier
of plastic bags and wearer of sensible shoes, walking
down the street of life: why can't I love you? Your
home is a furniture store, can't write my name on
any surface, the mahogany cabinet proudly gleams,
a polished brass key in its lock tells of cherished,
if useless, possessions. What a perfect widow you'll
be, putting my picture on the mantle-piece, dusting
me everyday, and go on living as you always have,
busy cleaning something.

To Be A Horse

After rain the pretty way is deep green; I'm
driving through a landscape eight shades
verdant. If I were a horse I would happily
neigh, jump clumsily in the air, eat too much
and get stomach cramps. As it is I caress damp
grass with my heart and wait for late January
when the almond flowers blossom. Pink, it
goes so well with green.

Almost Africa

In the unregulated, uneven stony landscape around here just before the dale ends in a nave, a dried up little lake looks in the evening haze like the African savannah. The sun sets early in December, but still manages to paint the sky blood-thirsty crimson, a colour that, if it appeared on black asphalt near a smashed car, would have looked gruesome. For now everything is beautiful. I see zebra and gnu graze and, in the tall grass, yellow shadows of hunger stretch and sonorously growl.

The Seagull

On a diving board, fastened to a cliff, I jumped
into the sea. Green bubbles gurgled in my ears.
When I broke the surface the board and cliff had
disappeared and I was alone in the middle of
the ocean. As I lay floating calmly on my back,
a seagull came and sat on my belly. We didn't
communicate, but its silence was better than
the vast ocean's. It flew away at sunset, had
seen a bigger object: a blue whale. I spoke to
no one except the night and my conscience. In
the morning both of them had gone. It was
noon when the Japanese harpooned me; luckily
they had a doctor onboard.
On top of the ship's mast the seagull sat, winked
once, but didn't smile. It had seen a bigger object:
a cruise liner balancing along the horizon.

John Thomson

Suburbia in Excelsis

In suburbia
that fabled land
where bungalows grow
and hedgerows grand
are never tarnished
by a working-class hand
in suburbia excelsis.
Where herbaceous borders
grow like rashes
the Holy Grail
of the middle classes
and excitement's always
served in glasses
in suburbia excelsis.
Where respectable sisters
of respectable families
will entertain ministers
not only on Sundays
nothing is sinister
except his homilies
in suburbia excelsis.
The last resting places
of aged bank managers
and well-known faces
and assorted villains
who remove all traces
of life
outside suburbia
in excelsis.

The End of Days at 3am

The clock ticks my life away,
as November yawns
and drizzles indifferently, in
the fog that chokes the streets
drifts and fades in alleyways
where lovers meet
and stop at grinning windows
where a post-box stalks souls
and winds past the bones of a graveyard.
It pauses there and listens hard
for sounds of the approaching dawn
and seeing there are none
gathers itself and carries on.
Somewhere deep in this infinity,
you begin again.
Without me.
There is stillness
in this room
that fills my senses full
of your absence.

Ships

Arrange the scene
of a seaside town
with onion air
where narrow streets
of sea-shell shades
and fish-shops bulge
with staring eyes
and sea-gulls scream
obscenities
and sawdust restaurants
stretch on and on.
To the chaos
of a fair
the shouts and screams
and two-for-a-pound
and unbearable
shapeless music everywhere
reach the beach
at last, where
the sun bakes the sand
and where
he slowly takes her hand
to journey to this end, and now
is as it should be
through browning bathers
the afternoon sleeps peacefully
past cunning sand-castles
where sky and sea
and Fife are one
and gradually they become.
Something new.
Someone else.

Cry of Love

The night is a stranger
slowly unfolding grief.
Cruel and precise as needed
it breaks on this wasteland
where no sun shines and
barren rivers have run dry.
In jagged shards of memory
the deep night softly whispers
I have seen Christ crucified,
Buddah dying in a gutter,
I have held humanity
I have heard her utter
Weep now, my Son of Man
Eloi Lama Sabachtani.
The night aches.
Somewhere far from here
a cry of love escapes...

Here, there be Dragons

Night threw its cloak
around the bed
covered the lurking demons
and said:
"Time to sleep, if you may
forget the guilt."
Three o'clock
the silence spoke:
"What is that shadow
by the door?
Why does it lurk
in the dark?
Who is it for?"
The clock struck four.
"Time to sleep, if you can
forget the guilt."
The silence sadly shook its head.
The silence said:
"You persist in resisting
being yourself.
Who are you?"
I thought of a crow
on a fence once.
An old black crow
still bright of eye
who winked at strangers
as they passed by.
The clock never reached five.
Damp sunlight stretched itself
around the room
flicked fingers into corners
embraced the brittle borders
and said it was noon.
Two strangers met again.

Desire

In a hollow skull,
as raw heat screams
of death and hell,
a phone softly sings.
I am not cruel
and speak only truth
in this paradise
of barren bones.
Here are pale shadows
still full of night.
They drift past slowly
in a perfume trail.
Too-thin fingers
lend tiny caresses
to dishonest men
with bloodshot eyes.
They search for gifts
from too long ago
as the phone sings
in praise of you.
Turning to go,
I am a stranger.

Beginnings

When wild bluebells dance
in perfect time and hold
green fingers to the sun
in brittle ghosts of grass,
they beg an azure sky
for rain.
A cold-eyed morning wakes
in crimson clouds
and crystal air.
Silence lasts forever.
On flames of green
as ravens cry
I take your hands.
They yield like
flowers in spring.

Requiem on Main Street (Fatima)

The headlights did their best
to pierce the gloom
which ebbed and flowed
and choked the streets.
And the room
was all unmade – a jigsaw.
Where pieces
of the past had been mislaid.
And life now moved
to a jerky 20s beat
as the rain danced
softly in the street.
And pale blank faces
will look up
emerge from a coffee cup
and listen to an anecdote
before reaching for a coat
and standing on a doorstep, fumble
for words to fit, finally mumble
"Goodbye" and turn and leave
a silence fit for any grave.
But not an end
just a change
at the most.
Say boy to man,
say girl to woman,
say Father and Son
and Holy Ghost
and admit defeat.
The wind crept slowly
down the street
and still the rain sighed.
Out of the depths, O Lord
I have cried…

Waiting Room

Wednesday is the saddest day
loud in their discontent
is a passing clutch of handbags
in a loud gossip of women.
The day is a snivelling man
in a coughing, shuffling stain
of wrinkled grey raincoats
taken root and slowly rusting.
Stranded in the embracing days
of here and now. Thin laughter
winding weakly down cool passageways
mocks time and age. And after.
Is God there? In that crumpled air
of shrunken faces
and grey shrivelled hair
with the watching windows misting?
In an antiseptic silence,
It is said he was seen once
when he stood outside entranced
eyes unsure
and waiting
always waiting.

Rome

Some day we will visit Rome again.
Brave the awesome summer thunder
to throw coins in the Trevi fountain
and drink strong coffee in cafés, under
rain-soaked sunshades. Watch as the
birds soar gracefully over the sunset
in St Peter's Square. The shadow
of the Coliseum will absorb late
afternoon glare. Today, there is only
an antiseptic ward and a kindly young
man who does not know what to say. Rome
waits for now in an unknown mist. Some
other time we will return, you say.
Another time, I promise. Some other day.

Ten Years After

In the wastes of suburbia
time is the common enemy
as unknown weeds and stress cracks
grapple pebble dash normality.
Beyond the brick red rooftops
the grey fog which lives near
the boat infested canal
smiles grimly in the smoky air.
The room is now rearranged
bed moved, lamp gone, colder
than usual. Nothing much changed,
only me. And I have grown old.
The downstairs morning bustle
intensifies. Early as ever, prompt
and punctual. The small window brings
breakfast smells from coffee stalls.
The black clothed Sunday silence
crawls empty streets and disperses
in the stony bells of a churchyard
and the past slowly, slowly emerges.

Market Values

It was a Saturday, I remember.
A mid-70s market morning. Light rain
slowly falling on wooden bric-a-brac.
We wandered in a grey September.
The smell of the overdone hot dogs
mingled with candy floss. And ragged queues
soon formed, long and disorderly, for
football tops or cheap new shoes.
By then we had passed the antique stall
the months of polishing hid the defects
and you told me you were very bored
or bland tactful lies to that effect.
I shrugged, I think, and it was done.
A simple act, the blank kindness of
opening a door for someone
who had just outgrown me. I felt numb
and watched the families pass. Bored
fathers, flushed mothers, children pushing
and no-one else seemed to notice
that the world had just stopped turning.
I visited the market yesterday
believing that I had myths to debunk
or ghosts to exorcise. I don't know.
But it rained and they still sell junk.

Alice, by the window

Alice, she
spends her days by hooded windows
with vistas of the past
slowly counting heartbeats,
watching gathered sparrows.
Old age
invades and suffocates
and grows
in the stony face of bungalows
and footsteps rise
like Lazarus
in brick red walls, wrought iron gates
past genteel cups and china plates
and the trees are restless.
Death intrudes
in dancing streets and cocktail bars
the hands that move past silent faces,
the hands who know the secret places
reach conclusions and solutions.
There is
dust here and silence
twists this darkened room
as the day descends
among yesterdays
and lilac blooms
congeal the air,
the click of needles
fall and rise and
fall in desperate
rhythm.
The drawing near...
and Alice does not stir.

Clive Warner

Bed Doddy

Sleep, bed doddy, sleep, and dream
of disposable razors, soap, lying naked
for Nurse Tronco with her magnifier,
her powerful lights, her twitchfingers

Climb on here, enjoy needle moments,
sleep, while electric scalpels part skin,
fat, and muscle, hissing steam rises
jigsaw teeth bite into pale white bone

Sleep, don't dream about jigsaw teeth,
blades, the split sternum drawn back
by an Octopus, blood dripping from
hung plastic bags on metal stands

Wake, but don't try to speak,
luminous green cathode ray tubes
display tracks from your heart,
urine trickles silently into bottles

Listen as beeping seconds tick off
time, using you as their clock.
Drain yourself slowly into plastic
tubes emerging horribly from skin

When the Foley catheter comes out
you will shout, but not as loudly
as you shouted when they dragged
the drain tubes from your thorax

You never read warnings on packets
or if you had, it would be someone else
lying here, not you, naked
under sterile drapes, bed doddy

She

When I first saw you on the floodlit catwalk
I felt passion stir and had to be in
your warm leather embrace.
While I was so in love,
I could not see your faults.
Proclaiming only virtues
I allowed photographs,
videos even, to be taken
which show a grinning fool:
I, with you, then.
The money I spent:
your black vinyl bra, body waxing,
silicone enhancements, rubber gear
– o God all that stuff.
But time passed, the mirror cracked
reality peered through your Metalflake skin,
a basic blush primer.
I should have known the clear coat
was an optional extra.
Despite my devotion you became frigid,
leaking body fluids.
In that menopause I sent you to another.
You came back purring and I was so happy
for you, me, us, then.
Even as you aged, losing your curves
I aged too, forgiving your lack of speed,
a slight sagging, the odd squeal,
even moments of total abandon
others remarked upon, winking,
thinking it me, not you.

But your emissions increased
former friends called hotlines
with ugly rumors:
you started smoking
and I lost you.
And so we part,
me in tears, you in parts.
Yet we may meet again,
incarnate in another life,
recycled, poor old car.

Eco-taxis

Green eco-taxis gather at night
under grey concrete bridges
metal woodlice mount each other
flash mirrors bump fenders rub wheels
stick exhaust pipes into each other.
Radiators boil over, steam rises
oil drips amber from sump pans
transmission fluid leaks past seals
green water trickles from radiators
cooling systems fail in heat.
Ochre flakes fall from dented bodies
headlights wink in the darkness
turn signals blink red yellow red
springs relax tiredly under seat covers
taximeters explode in blue sparks.

Fax Man

I open curled fax-paper wings
flap uselessly from the ragged sofa
just a time circuit transmission.
Original's back there in a mansion
with a supermodel a yacht in Cannes
a Maserati in Monza and laughing
all the way to the toilet 'and no damn paper'.
I see him like a quasar billions of light years
away, but the brightest thing in heaven.
I went wrong thirty years ago
picked up the phone seconds
early, stepped on a yellow beetle.
My original split off, let the phone
ring. Jain-like he donated a lifted
foot to the yellow beetle. Ripples
spread money passed from hand
to hand he didn't buy magazines
with can't fail investment offers
put it in Genentech and Microsoft
instead but I, the shadow, bought
stocks to repair my fading image.
Miracle cures and hair therapy
don't work on Xerox copies.
For a while I was A4 size
but now even that looks good.
The last letters fade away and I see
him nodding into his dream of my
nonexistence.

Total Body Transplant (TBT)

Of course he's getting younger
with Helena's liver, Wieslawa's pancreas,
just like the other wrinkled young men
watching MTV in the recovery ward
in the private private clinic
with the special special doctors
behind the green brass-studded door.
Of course, Mr President, we're lucky.
All those states voted for the death penalty
with very good results from the injections.
No tissue damage found.
And in your case, have you considered
a fresh prostate from a young serial rapist?
It could do wonders for your libido.
It's too humid, I think, for Guadalajara,
and they might recognize you there.
But of course, there's always Bangkok.
Oh, and here's some good news
the clone is doing just fine
and in your case, have you considered
a total body transplant?

Nopalitos

Cloud over Cerro de la Silla; lightning
or is it just strobe lights on TV masts?
There's a background muttering in the air
or is it just tyres on Las Torres?

Crickets chirp or is it just corrugated iron
and the wind?
Frogs burp deep in throated melodies
or is it garb deposits near depositos
farting gentle methane evening breezes?
Tired baby carrying indian women
eat bean taquitos invoke Quetzalcoatl
or Kukulcan or a dozen other
Gods that doze in reptilian pretence
of being in our likeness.

Rain frosts the air as cloud's first
caress kisses your brow, breathing
'you're still alive'.

Stones move like tortoises.
Darkness hovers just out of reach,
poised over your left shoulder like
some old najual waiting to recruit
you as the next Carlos Castenada.

Exhale that first sweet secret breath,
slowly expand and fill up spaces
in tiny drops of water in which you
exist waiting once again for lungs, a
voice with which to preach in vain
the folly of eating flesh.

Soaring like ragged eagles, gaps in cloud
allow the moon to pierce you in limelight.
Something perches lightly just under
your left eye and for the moment you
are unable to do anything as it
inches slowly but inevitably towards–
Ah God! The moment comes,
a sudden spastic sweep of hand
the creeping thing is gone and
outside an indian woman's voice
shouts "No–pal–it–o's?"

Nopalitos:	*Nopal cactus chunks.*
Cerro de la Silla:	*largest mountain of Monterrey, Northern Mexico.*
Las Torres:	*a main road running south of the city.*
depositos:	*shops that sell beer & soft drinks.*
garb:	*short for garbage.*
najual:	*Indian brujo, or wizard. Man of power.*

Procaration

It's unnatural without the right body parts.
Pipes always wrong, so they try it different ways.
Side to side. Doggy style. Head to head.
Broken eyes left lying in the road.
I tried to steer my Escort from predatory lovers.
They want to mount her, leave stains
at night, glowing green-yellow.
Today she betrayed me.
Slight drizzle and light fog concealed his approach.
Looming from sodium haze the Ram bellowed.
She gently tooted invitation, sidled toward him.
In vain I tried to divert her attention.
Her injectors took over. I spectated.
Coy, she rotated her bottom to face him.
His eyes pierced, he breathed oily aftershave.
With a triumphant bellow, he mounted her.
She shrieked, tiny body bent in macho embrace.
Later I went to the pound to identify her remains.
White-coated men came with a packing case.
Inside, a pedal car. The maker's badge said:
"Fordson" by Dodge.

Matachin

Red green plumes on your head
dance, dance, Matachin.
Grinning men in black glass Dodge Rams
see you dancing, hear your drum banging
for a peso in the downtown traffic.

Play your flute, Matachin
to the rhythm of snakehide drums
cut out hearts with obsidian blades
sacrifice drugged victims
splash hot arterial blood
in syringes given out by grinning men
in black glass Dodge Rams.

Push in the obsidian blade
push in the rusty sword.
Push in the needle
watch AIDs and brother heroin
smallpox and Cortes
Huitzilopotchtli and you:
come with heart, veins, soul.

Red green plumes on your head
dance, dance, Matachin
do you know the Jaguar Rain Dance?
Will you dance it for a peso
in temples where Nahua eyes stare?

Note: This poem is inspired by the matachin. This is a figure often seen in traffic, dancing with his flute and drum, dressed as a pre-Columbian Mexican indian. His precursors were the dancers, drummers and flute players who performed while priests cut out hearts from living prisoners. Nowadays this sight strikes me as degrading.

Monterrey

Trucks arrive in the early morning,
bringing babies for the Indian women
on street corners accosting drivers,
who sit blank-faced behind their black
glass windowed Dodge Rams, saying
no traigo, no traigo, no traigo, no …

One millisecond after the lights turn
green, horns blow, perritos blow
whistles in a special way they have,
pointing to the curbside, come here,
zona escolar, pay the multa or what?
while squeegeed drivers wag fingers.

Across roofs and gardens toot factory hooters
grinning tanned faces stream out of the gates
of Pemex, Vitro, Cemex, and Aceros,
into cantinas, ladies bars, and comedors
guzzling tacos, chorizo con huevo, Coronas,
frijoles, pulqe, tequila, and taquitos.

Distant sirens wail, perritos, firefighters,
public rescue; pilot fish around smashed
black glass windowed Dodge Rams.
Drivers hang out of windows, faces bloody
bodies impaled on steering columns.

While the baby-carrying Indian women stare.

Cenote

Champagne cenote, minnows frolic
streams of bubbles rise
fish lips nibble tiny morsels
sandwiched ham and cheese.

On the edge they sit, the tourists,
listening to their ghetto blasters
tuned to the max, acid hip-hop
Jeffrey, Dawn, Jane and Peter.

Signals come from distant pulsars
calling to their stoic subjects
dark obsidian-daggered people,
long extinct their bloody sects.

Minnows frolic, sandwich-sated,
in the golden shafts of light
glad that tourists come more often
than winged serpent's tasty bites.

Eyeless sockets gaze at minnows
gaze at tourists, unaware.
Rest in peace you ageless virgins
skeins of tangled jet-black hair.

Now the ball court beckons, and
taking out his brightly beach ball
Jeffrey hollers 'kickabout'.
Sacrilege in ancient halls.

Foot drawn back to kick for goal
Jeffrey freezes in his stride
hearing distant pulsars echo
nowhere now to run and hide.

From the ballcourt to the temple
Mayans took them to the altar.
Two by two, boys and girls,
virgins for the knife that sunders.

Ruby red replaces ham
as the heads begin to sink
minnows frolic, buffet lunches,
stains on stones, lovely pink.

Kukulcan sits and listens
to those tunes from distant pulsars
watches, as the wheel of life
brings more tourists from their parlours.

High Tide at Hightown

Smell of shit comes in with wind and surf
scummy yellow tidelap inches up the beach
castaway animals smile in pink and black poly
drowned dolls wave one-armed from the ripples.

Sand innocently absorbs careless cars
gulleys secretly fill behind you
someone lurks naked in the dunes.

Distant fog-buoys sound melancholy in the estuary
sea thistles shove purple crowns through flotsam
and some idiot broke all the green bottles
just like you did as a kid.

Mersey

In The Rising Sun, nursing a pint, argue religion
and see through the window, one-legged pigeons.
Shanghaied out of Liverpool; condoms offshore
here's a grog, lad. Swab the decks, Jack Tar.
Keel-hauled mate, master at Pier Head, thrown bread,
gulls in the wake, green lights and, in a floating shed,
Jolly Jack sings a briny shanty. Two men carry him out.
Barometers fall in pelting silence; Old Murphy shouts.

Sail for Rotterdam, ready forward ropes,
cast off in Birkenhead for a voyage of lost hopes.
The mate sees diving tars, an albatross with dolphins
flys the Jolly Roger, toasting shipwrecked captains.

Shanghaied sailors vomit foam; the hull trembles,
inviting ruin to Liverpool homes. Now leaving:
fifteen men on a bottle of rum. Swing the lead.
Bar doors open, Murphy capsizes: grog fills his head.

Meat pies sing echoes of river smells
sewage à la carte, served at eight bells,
shoulder parrot and glass of ale in hand.
Of course it's all a problem with your glands.
By stone pillars a bobby checks. The Mersey gurgles,
pulls wooden beer barrels back to pubs, burgled
in the night. Sailors watch engines in the turning tide
a barge thumps, rolls; the river rises, slips either side.

Dead man's hulk ahead. Yellow arms grab ropes,
captains laugh as they Shanghai drunken blokes,
bilges wait for Chinese curries eaten after four
and we set sail for Dublin's loamy shore.

Shipping Forecast

Dogger, rising. One and a half miles. Light.
Eight bells. Sea state calm, no life-vest
North North West, veering to West
Orkney, steady. One mile. Water tight.
Green the waves, the engine's ready,
Light. North, steady.

Dogger eight, North Orkney green light.
Rising bells North, steady.
The North, one sea west, one wave steady.
And state, veering mile, the A.
Calm to water engine's half,
No West, tight, ready miles,
Life light vest.

Fort Crosby

Holes fell from the sky to make
these ponds where crested newts
hide in rusty tins and
caddis-fly larvae hunt below.

I caught tadpoles, took them in glass jars
with pondweed to a concrete blockhouse
and smelt salt-marsh estuary breeze
in sand dunes blowing eye-grains.

Through cement-slit windows
across green glistening mud flats
I saw skeletal ships resting
deep in peat graveyards.

The jars have gone murky
only one tadpole left bits
of others float, accusing.
I made glass holes for them.

Shadows raced over rabbit warrens.
I looked up, saw giant four-engined
gulls carrying holes to make ponds
for kids in other lands.

Kathryn McL Collins

Higher Standards

There is nothing to fill me
but desserts and cashews
lately.
Where is the discipline
those funny old nuns
taught?
Tied to repetition
I'll never finish with
an original thought.

Roofing, Writing & Tigers

(written to the tune of roofers' hammers)

Roofing and writing
What's the dif?
Every hammer blow
Makes me dizzy.

Every nail driven,
Every key pushed
Attempting shelter for
Bodies and souls.

Breathing the same air
As the tigers of earth
Sometimes makes me
Yearn for flesh.

While my pile of unread books
Speaks to illiterate
Dozing and innate lack of
Perseverance.

I build a fine roof and
Run the Serengeti
Until my hands and paws ache.

My roof is sturdy.
My meal satisfying.
My books unread.
My poetry unfinished.

Touch of Silk

I thought it was all I cared about:
the soul, the spirit.
On a clear night of loneliness
stars shine coldly ethereal.

Abstractions of life
anchored in flesh.
I abhor
not being able to touch you.

Yearning does not
blow in the breeze
like heather
or shore grass.

The salve of fever
is a cooling snow,
not some loving suggestion
of care.

Or is it?
I don't know today.

I write and I write
vacuously striving towards
another dimension
to balm this body of heaven.

Your hand on my shoulder
is worth all the poetry on earth.

Beautiful Dreamer

I was looking up the path
To a door I'd never seen
When billows of mist sucked me
Into a remnant-filled living room.
These relics were alive, sipping tea,
Reading literature and I, obscured in haze,
Took a place on a down filled loveseat
Of golden brocade.
Finally, just what I wanted: to be
Historically present in a salon
Of learnèd men and women of yore.
With a start, Henry yelled
"What's that mess on the loveseat?"
We all evaporated.

Danny Boy

The piper across the street plays it.
A procession follows the dreadful box,
and trucks drown lament
in unforgiving noise.

Death is no ordinary excavation site,
yet provides jobs too distasteful for some.
Bring on the entertainment.
Danny Boy,
the pipes, the pipes
are barely audible.

A new house is being built down the block.
The workers are on the clock
and don't stop
for funerals and pipers.
Only for weather.

Wish You Were Here

Wait for me in the evening
and I'll come as the sun
melts into its earth on the
other side of nowhere.

Give me a sign so
I will know it's you
in the uncertain fade
of the shadow hour.

Call to me;
for I, a sore-throated
puppy whimpering for your regard
have no recourse in finding you.

Would you come to me
and caution me to clear my page
of heartache in knowing your pain
is over?

Many times your final moments
visit me but many times we are
locked together fluid … distilled…
so often laughing, sweetheart.

So often laughing, that tears
undistinguished joy from sorrow
roll seeping through my lips;
invading me with your life, your dying.

And I –
lingering in recall
sink solemnly into recollections' futileness
and abruptly drop off the edge of belief.

Some Day

After the
air settles
around me,
my lungs,

refusing to
fill or
empty,
however that goes,

and the noise of life
is silenced;
finality
will rid me of self.

Winter Wood Bares the Sky

Woods, you are earth's grand salons,
trees bare like basketball players
sent to showers still shedding sweat
descended from a topaz sky
that's only seen in winter.

Upon a burned out clearing
the sun shines brightest,
as it should be, when, but for
the intermittent squirrel chirp,
the only sound is wind, and orphan

leaves swooping like paper airplanes
colliding on a runway of sticks and stones
or maybe the sound of one hand clapping
to the tune of the occasional falling tree.

Snow Snatched

We encircled her
that February day.
Amid sustaining whir
she lay.

Had I known
ill emptiness to come,
I'd be there, still
hearing the hum.

Her feet were cold.
I tried to warm them.
She lay so still.
Mine own sweet gem.

Her brain, they said,
beyond all function.
The friar led the
extreme unction.

Oh, damn that day
with its bright big sun.
We loved the snow.
Now look what it's done.

Daylight Savings Time

Save not day's light for
another hour to shine
upon the stone's cold
replacement of your radiance.

Save not day's light for
another hour to shine
upon what is nevermore
that once was vibrant.

Save not day's light for
another hour to shine
upon your pictured smile
that's cemented in another time.

Save not day's light for
another hour to shine,
for darkness is surely here.

Ode to the Poets

I'm reading a book called
Shaken and Stirred.
It's filled with windows,
crystal telescopes
to my inner space.
Lines placed like violets
in a procession to the virgin,
poignantly penned
to shake and stir in me
the sun and moon
of my soul
borne by
words of strangers
who reflect that which
hides in the
marrow of my
degrading bones.
How do I thank
Them
for exposing me?
Exposing me to
their inner light
of hope and universal identity.

It Started With A Kiss

I remember with roseate eagerness
youth's joyful repetition.

Do your lips smile in recall
of the first time yours fell
silent upon them,
eyes shut in serene spaces?

Wandering flesh
from that moment on
until delivered in embrace here
to retrospective harmony.

I think sometimes of
how it used to be
when we were new
and I was pink
and you were blue.

And my toes curl
and my eyes water
and I know
the joining of souls.

Sobering Thoughts

I always come to this place
cast in marble solitude.
Wraith of the past
shimmies supernal through my veins.

Feels like stepping
into craggy-edged foam
as satisfying as
biting into a head of beer,

or maybe not.
At least the hops
do their temporary trick of
rendering me insentient

as the netherworld reaps
randomly for life
in hopes of ordering the
labyrinth to bring me false peace.

Batting Zero

My tangy tongue
breaks into
soul stealing sop
sad plush paranoia

until a fellow
word whistler
simply slides
into the home of my heart

with all the ease
of Willie Mays.

Music Returns You

Limp lay violin's strings
when not tuned.
My heart is lain flaccid
for not sighing

Whatever dirges
or begone lullabies
mortared the cobbles
whereon your aura is built.

I, to the tune of
some bow in tow,
remember days
of singing love songs

designed not for lovers.
Pledges of another kind
that mothers to daughters trill
reel in my immortal soul.

Fly off. I know you must
to whatever the trust
is now. And I will sing aloud
to your bluebird sister

as she dusts her nest
with ballads of her own,
using leftover notes of your love
too long ago lodged in her heart.

Dazz Jackson

M-L-B

He's such a mischievous child
Always gets into this and that
Can't ever tell him no
He'll interpret that as an open invitation
Got the eyes of a wide-eyed hungry tiger
Who said little girls are smarter?
I swear, I can see the mechanisms of his mind churn
when things just don't make any sense
I've watched him make timely decisions an executive
would wish he could make under the same sort of pressure
Hail to this bright-eyed inquisitive man-child's
Soul so pure
Mind yourself, or they end up minding you
Give them knowledge … endless amounts of wisdom
Out of their mouths come unheard-of solutions
Feed their bodies as you feed your empty stomach
Watch them grow
Watch them grow
into a
better
U

Unconditional Love

I need unconditional love
As I think deeply my mind falls
Into a smoky and cloudy fantasy
Uncertain of what to expect
I envision myself by myself.

I need unconditional love
What do I do about this sickness?
Lord God show me who cares
Or am I just another modern day
Shakespeare shedding eternal
Tears

I need unconditional love
Down on my knees, hands to the sky
Begging you please
Send me someone to love
Send me someone that will love me
Send me someone that would fight for me
Send me someone that will happily be my wife

I need unconditional love
When shall this end and will she ever come to me
Or am I just a fool waiting, anticipating,
All for the wrong one?
There's no shame in my game
Cause I can honestly say
I need someone to show me unconditional love
In return, I will show the world that love
Is the biggest threat of them all

That is Unconditional Love

a little boy's bad dreams

Picture him running through Armageddon
with church clothes on.
Can you see him trying to hold the roof
from falling on his head?
Once again, trying to save his world.

Holding him in your arms
shouldn't have been that hard.
Please don't leave me, he'll never say
but he still feels the pressure of the world
on his shoulders.

It's not that bad is what he tells himself
but the pain of living without a father's love
is so great, a little boy just can't concentrate.

Yes, this dream of his continues.
He sees and feel things you can't, and only to
a nice mellow can he write about it.
The sun charges his spirit before that animal
Inside takes over.
The little boy used to have puppy
eyes, now they're wolf's eyes.

Money, weed and women, is what he thinks about now?
God save him from your prison of evil. Save him from
your cycle of destruction.

Time goes by slowly for some.
People and places change.
Even you have changed.
Still he decides that he is the lamb that needs to be sacrificed
For his daddy to fully commit.

Father if this is so,
I too give myself to you
Cause I too
Love you daddy.

My Prophecy of Love

Finally, the time has come for us to be
so take my hand and walk with me
hold me tight, and then we shall see.

So let it be known
I've turned over every stone
talked on every phone
remembered each and every moan.
Love and fools, forever sharing the throne.

Run That Game

Before the Mack act
I came off rather strong
Aged long
Don't get ah brother wrong
I enjoyed our sexual song

Boy how it came along
You singing that sweetest of song
In the end
thought about it all day long

Of course, you and I assumed that I was strong
not to mention, headstrong
in the end, I was just tagging along
brother thinking he might belong

now here I sit, all alone
feeling all sick
thinking I was your ultimate pick
should've told me, I was nothing more than a good
trick

My Encounter With Sin

I don't know if you'll understand this … but here goes
I had lunch with a man whose name starts and ends with sin
He gave me five thousand in cash
Put in right there in the center of my hand

Afterward, he took me downtown to the IBM building so that I could meet with what
he assumes is the girl of my dreams
Yeah, she likes to read the scripture
Mr Langston, Mr Wright, and even Mr Ellis
Seventy thousand dollar a year hoe

Sin says she'll make me happy after I do him this little favor, you know
In the past, I avoided him so that I would grow
My little boy, man he just doesn't know
Thinks I'm a hero, even when I feel like a zero

Sin says, he'll even buy me my Range Rover!
Black or white … gold if you like
Got me an apartment too … 250 a month … I won't even hafta pay for six months
Says his sister will even watch my little boy while I'm out working

Damn … is this a life changing masterstroke
Or am I just tired of being broke
Sin handed me five grand today baby
Said that should help me out …you know, get me out of my hole … restore my
ego … my once high flying pride

That girl at the IBM building is supposed to help me forget
You … forget you
I'm scared baby
I'm scared because I'm tired of failing
Tired of wanting

All I need to do is to take this wee little trip to North Philly
Home of the trifling
I'm the only person that can do what he wants me to do
Five grand … I need to tell him something by six

What should I do
are you scared too
I'm so tired of not having everything but you
so fed up with being … whatever I am these days

If I had that five grand before I found out you were expecting
I'd be a father … a real father
I wouldn't be so ashamed of myself right now
so sad
so very sad

The Lie

Don't teach me how to read
Before you teach me how
To think
Don't explain love to me
Until you show me the advantages
and disadvantages of hate
Don't tell me and mines that we are all equal
when you know that equality is something
you earn, and not given.

Grandfather

I can remember a time when
everybody I knew,
knew me, or of me.
I can remember a time;
A simple time,
An easy time,
when your neighbors smiled and said "hi!" for real.
I can remember a wonderful time
when moms and dads would dance a jig for no reason.
I can remember a world that was so much easier to understand.
I can remember a time, a simple time when my feelings and concerns counted.
I guess I'm rather well removed from never-never land.
Because I can remember my elderly grandfather and his long talks,
his serious warnings,
his uncontrolled laughter.
Most of all, I can remember his pains and his loves.
I can also recall his vivid recalling of war:
The senseless destruction,
The mass loss of life.
His dark brown tired eyes never looked so distressing,
so far-away.
Is this what happens to
The peasants
The fore-wishers
The youth,
I ask you:
Is this how we all end up, when its all said and done?
Were my grandfather and his grandfather friends tainted with
Such sadness?
If so...
Why?

My New York Adventure

Dedicated to those who live and those who died in NYC

New York City
with all its moving and unmoving
bright lights
is about forty-five minutes
away
Flying high, as I get high
I haven't even thought about the role I shall play once I get there
Let's see
Will I be that down Nigga, or
that straight up in your face, clown Nigga
Maybe I'll be that, take a step back, cause I'm big as Shaq, Nigga
Oh I know, how bout that, around the way Nigga
Love to make a sista's stray
On da' real I ain't in the mood to be sexed up
I'm already messed up … with
loving X, Y and you too Z'er
Wisely, I digress
My son is mad … and damn near obsessed
"I'm all alone again," he cries
eyes aglow
he isn't feeling my flow
Growing up can be such a pain
Thankfully, his Mom can maintain
Cause having a father like me
Can be such the strain
Right before I left
I kissed him and his flawless butter pecan complexion
"I love you Daddy … I really do … if you don't believe me,
man, ask my shoe."
truly, he's my true reflection.

"I know baby, I know."
Nevertheless, out the door I went
On the way to the airport
I thought of U
Not X, Y or Z
Yeah, I'm that prototypical Nigga
Always dealing with many others,
however, none of them can kiss like U
None of them can keep a brother humble
Even if it means it'll take a rumble
Twenty-five minutes into my flight
I'm thinking about everything we did last night
Kissing
Biting
Yeah, it was all so inviting
Even if it was only to excite
it was one hell of a night
Flying high, as I get high
I scope this long legged lady scooping a brother out
Man, all she wants if for a Nigga to dig her out
Of course, I'm already messing 'round with X, Y, Z.
"Excuse me, but is it really that hard to see?"
I'm sorry; but your heart will never belong to me
Cause I'm just to busy dealing with X, Y and Z
Move on; move on Black man
Flying high, as I get high.

The Last Thought

Dedicated to those who have made the ultimate sacrifice.

It ended so quickly.
Can't even remember what caused me
so much pain.
God knows, your bright shiny face was the last thing I saw
before I fell.
Your touch – your smooth as a butterfly touch – was the
last thing I sought;
the only thing I needed.
Of course I fought the good fight
As I lay here … fading…
Fading…
Fading…
Suddenly,
I heard someone say
"You're a hero, Private."
"People back home are gonna remember your name till the end of
time."
"I swear, they're gonna name a street after you boy."
"Are you serious … a street?" I choked out as my heart tried to stay
here … here in a world that seemed to be so full of hate.
Wiping away the warm blood that covered my face,
this no-face, I heard him whisper,
"yeah son, right there on Broad Street … you know, where you used to
play as a kid."
"Oh yeah," I coughed out as the pain started to fill my entire body.
"Will she … you know … will my girl get to see it?"
"Of course, she'll see it son … she and everybody else will see it."
"Will it make her sad?"
"No son … it'll make her proud … you can trust me on that … I promise."
"Please … please don't say that word…"
"You didn't break your promise son."
"I won't see her again … will I?"
He slowly lowered his head as if he knew something I should know.

"They can have the street. They can even have my legacy."
Afterward, I swallowed hard as long tears full of blood and sweat ran down my face.
"I just want to see her again. I mean, I just wanna tell her how much I ...
how much I...
how much I love..."

Negro X

Back then
I refused to smile
I refused to accept
that non-violence frame of mind
Unlike others
I'll stand and fight with a closed fist
before I let you spit on me and mines
Know this if you don't know anything else, man without color
Forgiveness and revenge awaits for no man
be he black, yellow, or green
surely my awaiting fist will carry the night.

If God Could Talk To Children

Influenced by Langston Hughes, *God to Hungry Child*

Cry those tears, why won't ya
Lick those wounds, cos brother
you ain't got time for some Saturday morning cartoons

Aw'ight you dirty dogfaces, wipe clean those once youthful funny
faces
Tie up those shoeless shoelaces, cos I'm bout t' take you to a
worse place,
called your birthplace. Sorry, you won't be able to read about this
in some
dusty governmental bookcase

So disregard those hunger pains, cos that ain't my rain, raining
down
So stand up straight, and listen to what God hafta say

I didn't make this world for you
I made it for the rich
I made it for those over-achievers, who've achieved what it means
to be me
I made if for those who enslaved, raped and murdered in my name

Nothing's changed
Hurry up and learn the game
Which game?
The game you couldn't tame
My bad, guess I gotta explain

Do you own stock in this world wide game?
Do you pay taxes for no reasonable gain?
Can you show a real profit for your work and strain?
Can you rap, sing, or perform sexual acts for the normally disdained?
Do you own oil, gold, and salt without any historical fault?

You, the children of war
Can't you see
I didn't make this world for thee

Little Boy of Mine

This little boy of mine:
eyes and body so strong,
makes a King feel right at home.
This little boy of mine
will never know how I love him so;
even when he makes me mad:
eatin' candy at bedtime
sneaking in some pop when poppa said no;
still can't stop loving him so.
This little boy of mine
grows like the grass of tomorrow,
reaching for the sun in the day
and the stars at night.
How I love him so,
this little boy of mine.

Tom O Campbell

a heathen mourning

ghost of laundromat
queen puffs at the window
likes her work, gets to talk. was
in the navy. got out. covering
hickeys her specialty. two
kids hence she puffs folds and
wonders "what if." speaks of
allergies, where they'll be
stationed and vacation with
folks in california. today

is different. fresh meat
enters: middle-aged, wishy
washy. wide eyes and dreamy
smiles greet jerry springer-esque

i settle in then the pigs. buckets
of wet never looking up taking
over tables, carts, air. their bitter
lives dragging huge behinds.

i don't look up. eyes burn my
backside. a cauldron of the
needy wanting bitter, and
lonely. daytime TV starts early

if you know where to look.
today is father's day. talk of
sitting home alone
and the weather and car payments and

hoping for a drop off. men only
drop-off or pick up. never stay.
just like at home. here the bitter
you, my love.

Tonapah Rose

Pavement cooks, shimmers
sand, rocks, snakes, ravens
always ravens, endless
miles, only ghost town
off ramps. Too hot
for traffic. Too hot.

Next exit Tonapah
ten miles. Nothing else
for forty or more. One
gas station, a lone restaurant,
five room motel, states
NO JAIL on its caged

wall. Coffee, hon? from
nowhere. Sure, thanks,
from out of my daze. Strange
place, part general store, justice
of the peace, hunting license,
tow service, and food. Table

games, little boards with
holes and pegs, books with
prayers and helpful sayings
like you might need them at
any moment. She never
stopped. Big place, handful

of customers, cleaning,
refills, like a worker ant, always
moving. "What's down the road,
more town?" "Don't
know, only been here six
months." Smile minus two

teeth, but cute, kind, and
genuine. Next refill around:
"If you don't mind my
asking; how did you end up
here?"

"We just
had to get out of LA, you know.
Tire went bad in the heat, and no
money. Got a job at a truck stop,
till they went out of business. The
last ghost town. This, the
next off ramp up the road."
Been here six months. A raven

never stops, survives anywhere.
What is time? So exact,
but without boundaries.
A German tour bus pulls up in a cloud
of dust as I exit into the sweltering
heat from a hot flashback in time.

Suds

yes, the morning was light
like a diet version of the real thing
hot shower felt good as the thick
rich soapsuds on slippery flesh
missing was you standing in
footprints opposite mine where
you once stood as glistening
soapy bodies slid searching for
traction delighted in finding nothing
but another heart pounding through
each chest another mouth pressing
another loving us wet and dry.

One Headlight

a cocky, unfinished moon
hangs solitary
in the mottled southern sky
burning bright through
open window onto the bed
beside me
where you are not. the
sheets pull and tear at my
flesh with every restless move
in sharp
contrast to the velvet
smoothness of your skin
and whisper of your
gentle touch.
at first i was angry, this
mocking, sardonic moon, but
now realize: it's not laughing
but only as incomplete
and lonely as i.

Hark

what light through
yonder window breaks?
is it not the moon?
is it the not the sun?
fear not sweet maiden
for the steam is thick
and the doors are locked
it is only a flashlight
in the setting sun and
we have this flannel
sheet and the barest of
us the strongest of love
that pounding must be
our hearts for it grows
louder and louder with
every magical thrust of
your hips, your lips
racing my body like a
test driver on the slippery
mountain road to my heart
our hearts, our love stronger
than any ray-o-vac beam
cold tombstones a cruel
waiting place on such a
cold and wet day a day
made for love for us
spent is not for the arco
mart or the shrimp basket
but for us not now not
while you fill me with a
thousand volt rushes and
liquid kisses and words of
love our moist love becomes
hot and gushes and shakes
and we kiss passionately and
start the motor and roll away

Curiosity and a Good Shove

was all it took to open this old house
tall, solidly built, aging naturally with
only minor signs of outward repair
many passed, but the house sat unnoticed

not vacant but inactive as if its time had
passed. not run down, but not in fashion
the knob shiny from use. the inside cold,
but somehow inviting despite the darkness.

shades responded to your touch. layers
of wallpaper each from a different time
pleasing a different taste once long ago
you carefully stripped away,

rubbed the worn wood, oiled an unknown life in
never before a home, a place for love. never before
open allowed to be itself. encouraged to be the
home it was born to be. my heart. your home.

Cabin Fever

coffee perks while weak
bulbs yawn and stretch through
pulled shades to light the cold
dark morning sky. cabin fever
unbroken. a deep white fluff lies
between us like deserts of fear
and loneliness pulling our towns
our tears yet even farther apart
these bodies hold memories of
fiery heat soft precious touch
smell of flowers that feel as
rosebud lips to caress this heart
longing, writhing, reaching,
searching like a lonely wretch
who blindly gropes for his
morning paper in the snow
where prints of paws meander
away from morning coffee chat.

tweet poem

this is a story i never want to end
two birds on a limb

peering through the brushes of life
mother nature ravages

and smiles. rain glistens on your brow
as the sun shines on us

large winged shadow protecting from burn
but the fire within

remains for you, day after day, hour after hour
my little chickadee.

Tomorrow and Tomorrow

growing anxious
to crawl
between the sheets
with you
in my heart

we sleep as one
your skin
elegant to be in
be still
my pounding heart

breathing loves
scent lips
poised tongue sweet
taste us
wet hot love

morning light soft
birds chirp
love's first sizzle
eggs bacon
juice of love

Words

of love and wonder
a glimpse of ice crystals
on frozen moss, perhaps
a pillow for wide-eyed
beauties in search
of a place to cuddle
for a night. they're
hunted for brains much
safer on trains. a
fat leaf impaled, caught
in flight like cupid's
arrow in freefall. wasting
not, with vision of our nest.
what time my love? our
time is always.

Nearly Seven

been thinking about a bathtub for two

warm water me and you.

we walked around the block just before dark

me minus you.

in some places sidewalks

covered with snow.

one stretch beside a naked hedge

had one set of human tracks

and tiny birdy feet.

human went straight.

birdies went crazy.

like me for you.

could've been

love birds.

me and you.

Understanding, a Poem

When will it start? asks
the cashier at the market.
Maybe by noon, I say. Wrong.
Severe weather storm warning,
the radio blares while I drag
drenched paper grocery sacks
from puddles on the truck floor.
Water, duct tape, plastic sheeting.
biological, chemical or nuclear?
the radio continues in monotone,
It's not if, but when. Prepare.
Your choice: duct tape, plastic sheet,
water, food, ammo, explosives,
understanding, a poem. Love.

Heather Grace Stewart

12 Months to Go: Bad Advice on Marriage

"*Love is grand;*
Divorce is 30 grand,"
The Old Mill's waiter laughed
and handed me
my piece of meat.

The Old Letch
said marriage
is like a car dealership
and raising kids is
only a business.

I think I'll stop asking.

On Being a Girl

I am 7.
I'm the best frog catcher
at our cottage.
I like building blanket houses,
lying on my back watching
cotton candy clouds go by,
giving my bear birthday parties.
I need my parents more
than my friends;
I like them more than my teachers.
I want to wear sparkly blue wings at my back
like the angels I play with.
I want to dance for no reason–
I don't need a reason.

I am 11.
The media calls me a Tween,
the economy loves me,
I'm supposed to want
everything sold in shades of pink.
But all I really want is to fit in and
into this awkward, gangly,
girl-becoming-woman body,
To find a place somewhere
between your complicated world
and my carefree dreams.
I don't really need a cell phone,
low rise jeans, or to
play that music you call 'noise'
quite so loud.
I just need
A hand to hold,
A listening ear,
To sleep with my teddy bear
when no one's watching.

I am 16.
Lunch time at school, I sit with The Girls:
angry, swarming bees
ready to sting at any moment.
Anything I say against the pack
will be taken back
to the Queen;
punishment will not be sweet;
I will hurt for weeks.
I like boys now; mostly because
our conversations run
deeper than "Where did you get
your lip gloss?"
Secretly, on weekends, I
spend time with my parents,
laugh more than ever,
learn more than
any day in school.
I can't wait to drive–
no place in particular,
windows down, fresh thoughts in–
away from the places and people
telling me who I should be.

I am 18.
I think I'm fat.
The fashion magazines
And TV makeover shows
Tell me so nearly every day–
I don't have the power to argue.
When I'm not obsessing
about fat or boys or whether
I'll get the car Friday night,
I'm actually interested in the world around me:
The war, why it started, will it ever end,
how many souls in far away lands will die for
our North American sins.
I attend protests and sit-ins for peace,
and actually believe

I can make a difference in this world.
Adults call me confused, but if they
would only listen to my ideas, perhaps they'd see
I am the future.

I am 32.
I'm my own woman,
but look to my mother and grandmother
as the women I want most to be like.
I'm still searching for answers, but know for certain
I want love and joy in my life, and to find a pair of comfortable jeans
that don't slide down my butt whenever I try to walk.
No more strappy shoes or tight boots on a daily basis:
I love myself too much now to torture my toes like that.
I play with my young nieces, revisiting the world
of blankets and bears,
clouds and cotton candy,
and feel a letting-go I've forgotten
or deprived myself of
for far too many years.
I own my weaknesses
and savour my strengths.
I have a place and a passion to call my own.
Every day I'm proud of the journey
that got me here.

Home

Here, in the shelter
of my lover's arms,
I am home.

Like disappearing
sand dunes on deserted shores;
sunny spots in the cottage woods,
sprinkled with white Trilliums;
childhood tree forts cradled in
towering pines;

I have a hiding place
here, on his chest,
here, in the crook of
his neck,

here, in the shelter
of my lover's arms.

Wedding Day

First sunlight falls
on a crisp, white gown,
then over my face
as I stir to recognition.
Eyes open,
breathing faster,
I sit up in silence
to watch the
wind whisper through
a floor-length veil,
and my heart rejoices.
Inside a small stone chapel,
we light the inner candle
but don't extinguish the outer two,
for in marriage, the minister says,
you must find the capacity to merge
without losing your individual selves.
"Two flames, one light,"
we say in unison,
and my heart rejoices.

Up the aisle
as man and wife,
tiny bubbles tickle
my bare shoulders.
His hand squeezes mine.
The organ plays a blissful tune.
Walking along the canal,
I stop to smell
my rose bouquet:
hepericum berries and greens–

all those pines climbed
as a child–
and my heart rejoices.

At our celebration:
cognac kisses,
his warm lips on mine.
The August sun beats down
but the lake breeze cools my skin
and dances with my veil
like clean sheets on a clothesline.
Our piper's song
meanders across the marina
as the wine fills our glasses
and the tears fill our eyes.

Later, we escape to the big dock
as sounds become distant:
muffled chatter,
giggles between kisses,
my feet making rings
in the water–
and our hearts
rejoicing.

The Gift

Asphalt-hot July;
feels like a sauna in the shade.
Sweat pours from my brow,
drips down my chest.
I carry a cumbersome bag of
winter clothes, unwanted,
five blocks from our home.
When I arrive, the local Seconds shop is closed.
I toss the bag into a donations box
that looks and smells like a dumpster,
and turn for home.
"Ahh!" cries a small voice from inside.
Startled, I look down to meet the eyes
of a malnourished five-year-old black boy,
so skinny, he looks closer to three,
his sad chocolate eyes deep-sinking.
He climbs out quickly, bag in hand,
and gives me a three-toothed grin.
"Mamma!" he says. I turn to face a woman
wrapped from head to toe in a purple African robe and
head-dress. "Mamma, she is giving away a scarf in her bag!
A scarf!"
'Mamma' looks at me, then at the goods.
Unsmiling, she wipes her sweaty,
soiled face with the back of her hand,
then asks, "You are giving away all this?"
disbelief in her eyes.
"Well, we need to make some space in our closets," I say,
shame caught in my throat.
"Here, then, son. You may have these."
She hands him my old scarf, tattered hat,
a pair of dark blue wool slippers.

His eyes grow bigger.
"Slippers!" he grins at me,
then puts them on his
tiny, bare feet.
"Are they really mine, Mamma?
For free, Mamma?"
Her pride allows her one nod, his way,
then mine. She turns,
taking his hand in hers.
He looks back and waves:
hat on head,
scarf around neck,
my favorite slippers on his feet.
"Thank you. Thank you for the gift!" he laughs,
and the blazing heat is forgotten.
In asphalt-hot July
I walk home
warm, empty-handed,
richer.

Child Soldiers

In Sierra Leone
the children cry
forced to watch
their parents die.
Young girls held captive
tied to a stake,
Turned sex slaves.
Amputated; raped.
Childhood is fleeting;
peace unknown.
But we're in the West.
Where's Sierra Leone?
Dead daughters, lost daughters,
lives of pain.
They run from their families
for fear of shame.
In Sierra Leone
the children cry,
and look to us
with empty eyes.

To learn how you can help the children of Sierra Leone, Africa, and those of other war-torn countries, please visit: http://www.theirc.org/childsoldiers/

Nine Lives

She's been married
nine times, she says
as she crosses her legs
and smiles at the
talk show shrink.
"I can always spot
husband material!"
she laughs, then
confesses that
after number five,
she started to
question
her abilities.

Maybe next time
she should
just get
a cat.

On Rainy Nights

On rainy nights,
dark streets sleek,
and you are late–
I hold my breath,
pace like a caged panther,
look out from our warm home
into the bleary black–
Stop, don't imagine the worst–

For there is much to be lost.

Away from you,
I flirt with freedom:
Controlling the remote,
I have a whole bed
to myself, eat
popcorn for dinner,
live for me alone.

And when I return,
You are always there,
in the darkness,
Waiting for me.
My heart still flutters
at first sight.
We hug and kiss
in the pouring rain–
not caring what others think–
holding onto what we have,

For there is much between us;
For there is much to be lost.

Priorities

Like the setting sun,
children laughing,
seashells in the sand–
the great Gerbera
blushing
in the chipped green bottle
on my desk
is a distraction;
perfect and pure.

Woven

My parents are getting older.
This, I just realized
along with the cruel crinkled lines
that circle my own eyes.
(A quirky revelation,
as if they were never aging before,
as if I'm telling them something they didn't know!)
They're also getting wiser–
Or is that just me?
Like a baby discovering
its own toes
for the first time,

I finally see
what had been there
all along,
only I was too stubborn
to dig deeper
until now:

I laugh out loud at my father's corny jokes,
finish my mother's sentences,
argue with my love about how to fill
the dishwasher right and
hear odd adages from my youth
mysteriously spurting forth
from my own mouth.

They are a part of me–
Inextricably woven into
my fabric–
So I will never
really
be alone.

Instinct

Golden sunshine shimmers
on this lazy lake
like sequins. A lone cormorant
flaps its wings incessantly,
as if in defiance
of the coming cold.
Oblivious couples walk
arm in arm beneath
the weeping willows,
kicking up dead leaves like
forgotten arguments.
They sport only T-shirts –
the joggers, shorts –
as if wearing them
will prolong
the inevitable: snow
sleet, heavy traffic,
Christmas crowds,
cell-phones ringing
in the middle of a movie.

The cormorant spreads his wings
and praises the sun,
preening on his rightful throne,
unaware that winter is late this year–
going by instinct
because that is all
he knows.

Autumn Will

The great oak sways proud, stands high,
Then paints its final will against an autumn sky:

That is how I wish to live, and how I wish to die.

Its branches like a lover's arms; its shadows where the lonely lie,
Where the old find shelter and the young learn to fly–
The great old oak sways proud, stands high.

Embracing change from day to nigh,
It bows to hold the children; uplifts all passers by–
That is how I wish to live, and how I wish to die.

Its last leaf falls with bright flamboyance,
A crimson battle cry! – and still
The great old oak sways proud, stands high.

Its branches have broken, its roots run dry,
Reduced to a stump, it asks not why–
Just comforts each friend that
comes there to cry.

That is how I wish to love, and how I wish to die.

Christmas Shopping

Empty boxes, empty wallets,
cups with cold tea left aside.

"Hurry up, wrap it up."
Fill that empty space inside.

Get ahead, get it first,
get it while it's still a trend.
No time for carols, nor for tea,
nor the beggar 'round the bend.
Cards with designs, get them pre-signed
when you don't know what to say.
Put it on credit. Already read it?
Back again on Boxing Day.

Empty boxes, empty wallets,
cups with cold tea left aside.

One Morning

This morning
we woke from our lovers' lair
to winter's first blanket
and frosted stars
on our windowpane.
So intricate, our little nova,
we forgot last night's words,
unpaid bills,
the threat of war.

Leafless oak trees,
now adorned with
shimmering garland,
greeted us like festive
Christmas firs.

In the park
across our street,
giddy laughter echoed from
inside snow forts;
behind enemy lines.

When the little people appeared–
pudgy snowmen with soggy mitts
and brightly coloured boots–
they fell to the ground, giggling,
making angel imprints–
Lifting loneliness from the hearts
of the park-bench people.

This one morning
we awoke to
laughter and a
fresh, white world.

John G Hall

The Manchester Blues of Night

The dancing cat fell. Mars made
soft tracks in space while my hand
unclasped from you. Shadows of
lovers shaped across blackness
by yellow light, while my love faked
rabbit legs behind my back. Pistol songs
banged from the jukebox, pierced tongues
bite for bite. But the safety of freedom
flops, cigarettes burn, electric shocks,
heaven being deeper than submarines can drop,
while hell closed for freezing over. We floated out
into the cool Manchester blues of night, Mars
left floating cold, a sodden cat in a city cut.

Since She Turned Remote

She used to come to me
and turn the control
till silence was gone.
But now she keeps a
comfortable distance.
I hardly feel the brush
of fingers, merely
the thick coats
of desire's dust
and the occasional
kicks of hope, now
my only pleasure
the sweet revenge
of fuzzy pictures
and missed episodes,
her faults my only solace
since she turned remote.

Universal Kisses

See how the moon
sucks on the sea
See how the sun
warms on the bloom
See how the star
lights from our eyes
See how the earth
feeds from our hands
Powers that come
Powers that go
Universe rocking
me to and fro
The cradle of matter's
spiralling arms
carrying on, bearing me up
into its blackness,
pressing me close,
smelling of whiskey,
weight twisting, pressing me
from out of the dark
like a stranger's tongue
tasting my mystery
singing my song

The Swings

A mother younger than
my Colin Bell pennant,
Mexico World Cup 1970,
pushes a blond boy
in a Hollyhedge park.
Slung between swings
the arc of his life is shot
but never dropped. Here
she puts his heart in her mouth
and stares out of the grey snap
at him and his city scarf
flying out towards the universe,
she whispers something
as if praying for his safe return
or at least an away win.

Last night, today & tomorrow

Last night I drank to one too many pretty women.
Last night I fed on a feast of friends.
This morning my mind is filled with lip-stick
and my memory is fat from remembering,
that the world can be piss stained and glorious
at the same time as the kind earth's head
be black-bagged and hung with hempen rope
like a black American found guilty of being poor.
Last night I kicked a door down to get to you.
Last night I picked you up so easily.
This morning you stink my room out,
an editor's corpse drunk dry and returned,
the words downed by one shot.
Where can a poet go now but out into the streets?
Petrol bomb poured, zip lighter cocked
flame flickering, the wick cool and blue
like the soul inside a burning monk.
Today you poured out one too few drinks.
Today you starved on a famine of loves.
This evening your heart is empty of kisses
and your dreams are thin from forgetting
that the moon can be fog bound and mysterious
at the same time as the cruel seas open and wide.
Be white winged and free on the soft warm blows,
like an African pearl asleep in the black tide.
Today you rapped on my mind like a top ten.
Today you picked me up so slowly.
This evening you scent my hiding place,
A writer's thirst sobered up and hidden,
the words found by your eyes.

Where can a poet be now but inside the moment?
Double whiskey singular, ice cubes floating
heat haze rising, the liquid red and black
like the bonfire of our love letters that autumn.
Tomorrow I will fill up one too many places.
Tomorrow I will gorge on a banquet of hates.
In this future my mind is full of faces
and my regrets are stuffed from promises.
That the sun will forever burn towards its end,
at the same time as the kind earth opens its hands.
Be black coal spinning in the hard cold of space,
like an American soldier at peace in a white desert.
Tomorrow you will calm me down like King Cole.
Tomorrow you will put me down so hard. That evening
will leave me losing everything, a writer's secrets
made obvious, the words written by your listens.
Where can a poet be then but outside futurity?
Cards dog eared, hot thoughts gambled
cold dice rolled, my falling cuts left bleeding here,
like the snakeskin of your devil hanging on my bedpost.

Another Poet On Another Plane

The fumble-fisted poet
full of Peregrine dives
plops to earth.

Full of immaculate wrongs,
weighing his words
with intensive breath,
and desperate concern.

When all he wants
is to screw the airhostess,
and experience yet more
significant knowledge.

Before his ink runs dry
and his nib curls.

Mingus

Mingus music waited in the string's
jump. Dust sat down and prayed
for fingers, thumbs and hits.
Loose gone tight, tight gone loose.
Blue loops gave him the notes to play
wrapped around him like girls' hips.
Dots like lost continents amongst the waves,
drops of black and white paying dues to Africa.
Jesus! Even Billy-clubs in the darkness worshipped.
After the booze the jazzed rage slid along
the hallelujah ropes, angel licking his soul,
devil clipping his wings, man shining up his shoes. Yet
the sounds sat it out, patiently waiting like death
until the storm before the calm poured down his gift,
Mingus music weighted in the strings.

Taste of Human

The child is
human sushi,
the adult
hard-boiled,
the old one
blanched,
free from
taste.

All that is
left to us,
is our
liquor, and
the final
straw.

Suck
baby
suck!

Before
the blood's
gravity
falls.

Leaving
all our days
tainted
by regrets,
aftertaste
after thought.

Some Words

Some words are placed for audience
the gravestone, the eviction notice.
The competition-winning anthology
of prescription, recipe and warning.

Some words are placed for effect
The 'fuck you' tattoo, the Oxfam badge.
The affirmation of self-deluded nihilism
of manifesto, ego and sexless sex.

Some words are placed for safekeeping
the priest's forgiveness, the cop's note-book.
The forgotten slip of the soul's tongue
of loose lips, oaths and public prisons.

Some words are placed for pain
the gun manual, the lovers' guide.
The powerful squeeze of male fingers
of triggers, truths and nervous kisses.

Some words are placed for minding
the boy abused, the woman raped,
the unfurling terror of king & queen
of chains, soft whispers and hard fists.

Some words are placed in secret
the damp earth, the poet's grave.
The poet's poem the ground disturbed
by letters, paper and the shovel of words.

Communion

My mother brings my father's god to him
in a small leather bag every Sunday morning.
God travels the road snagged in her pocket
smuggled past betting shop & doctor's office.

He travels through streets holy incognito
freshly cooked, dreaming of tasty souls
grace wriggling amongst her shopping.
A last meal served by a mother to some
other mother's son, a-ring-a-roses of Pietas.

God undressed, a white poppy rolled in flour
is eaten unseasoned by snaked tongues, power
and glory, going going gone! She turns the sack
inside out in case a piece of Jesus has hung back,
then tucks god's carrion bag in her top drawer along
with her sympathy cards and the comfort of crumbs.

My Belfast Bomber

I found a singer who knew my song
who loved the lyrics with her slender voice
But my fingers played too fast to follow,
squeezed too hard on love's hair trigger, backfired
at close quarters, my innocence a hidden gunner.
A sound in the soul that ricochets continuous
with the crack in the night, the powder flash
and the perfume of cordite. My last post played
on the torn bodhran of my sweet Belfast bomber.

Heather Bryant

Impressionable Skin

Lover, in case
I never mention it,

my impressionable skin
has grown thin

lips and hips and bony wrists
reflected in the mirror.

wait and stare
and contemplate.

been so long since we
laid down.

tonight, might be a speck
of someone

you don't remember.
don't know. different somehow

can't imagine
what you'll think

but I expect to be alone
at the end

Shot

Glass reflects the counter light,
transparent, waiting for first base.

Two liquid tongues meet for the first time
in a French twist kiss.

Bailey's an overseas cream boy.
Marnier's an elegant copper girl.

They swirl together
and meld in the glass middle.

Kalhua watches from above.
He joins the combination.

They reach for his coffee brown
and push him underneath.

All three mix and blend together,
one and a half inches, tangled.

Violet Skin

Random adjectives were printed out, cut into squares, pasted on walls,
scattered thoughts in Times New Roman font.

Lava lamps hovered over ashen faces and quivering hands.
With each daredevil, shadows quaked over the stage.

You were on the floor, directly in my sight.
I was as narrow and divided as my microphone stand.

Couldn't tell if you recognized me. I had knotted hair
and violet skin under the spotlight. A performer, poseur.

Then again, I wore the same blue jacket
once tossed over your bed in a long-lost April.

As I read a poem, I was curled inside, trying to breathe,
trying to say the words without stammering.

Beside the spotlight, you smirked in my direction.
You didn't blink once.

You knew what lingered under every vague word.

Dock Poem

the lily pads float
in drowned circles

like a bloated Pac-Man
retired from the arcade

white dragon flies
cling to the edge

and surf the treacherous tides
that start from my foot in the surf.

Music For The Quarantined

exhausted
back home.

alone again at dawn.
dishes stained.
dried flowers in vase.
brand new song on the radio.
i used to love this part.
the newness.
the unpredictable next note.
i go back at noon to plastic sheets.
a cold, sterile, bloodless body caught in a plastic net.
i want to wipe him pink.
i want him home.
or just gone already.

Old Silk Shoes

They are tight around my toes, these old silk shoes.
I haven't worn them in years, and yet I keep them
locked away in a drawer, the ribbons wrapped around
the arch, ready for the next recital.

I used to wear mine with Hanes Her Way socks
with a leotard and bike shorts. I liked bare legs, seeing
my calf muscles bulge in the mirror.

There is still lamb's wool in the toes, musty, gray.
I remember how to do this, where to stuff
the wool, where my feet hurt the most so I can
feel the least of it possible. I remember. I always
had one toe longer than the other, and it jammed
up into my joint, my single pain point. I was lucky,
I never got blisters or raw bloody feet like some.

I tie the ribbons, frayed at the edges around my ankles
and make a tiny knot. The securing elastic is concealed
under the guise of perfect pink ribbon.
I stand and flex my feet. They are not broken in,
nor flexible, but they'll do.

How is it that I used to do this?

How did I leap *en pointe* and linger
in concentration, waiting for the next beat?
I can barely stay on toe for a few seconds.
My ankles ache with the strain and my balance is gone.

I hold onto the edge of the wall, embarrassed. My feet
burn in the old toe shoes, as if humiliated.
I long for my old strength. I feel ancient at a
quarter century, an old lady in the dance world.
I'd be near retired by now, if I hadn't already.

Jordan

Three cheek freckles in a triangle,
wisp-dry hair, cardboard brown.
small white graceful

high school intellectual, always right.
She was a genius after all,
my best friend.

Seven years of hot debates,
green little me from the start
always wrong, always

the sidekick, young and sick,
trapped in petty secondary.
She had to be forgotten.

Nearing the End

Quarters rattle in his hand.
Interrupts the moment, the smoke

I'm trying to breathe in.
Stand on one foot, precarious.

Back in blue leather pressed against the wall.
arms crossed tight, waiting to go home.

Andy paces, watches the taxis fly, tries
a two-second icebreaker every five.

I make small town excuses,
avoid all answers.

Ouliette Avenue

There's an elderly man in a black car
crouched in the driver's seat
outside of Knox church.

His blue sweater tangled sideways,
he's not sleeping. Hiding a book
under the window, watching the bells.

A bongo drum at the Palace Cinema,
a guitar to the side. Two
femme heads bob in hippie rags

designer jeans, blonde spikes,
cranberry braids. Their case is wide
open and brimming.

'Find the way with Jesus!' he yells,
large black wobbly with cane, waiting
waiting for the 1C bus.

'No dieting' reads the pin on her hat.
She sucks on her gum, swings
the scarf around her neck

Girl, stunning with cigarettes, body's
musky perfume wrapped tight
in black cat suits. Pale, tangled, absent.

Leaving Mina

I sleep in spare sheets of hers
without scent,

Nothing but softness, her softness
soaked into fabric.

The soft of her body, the cheek I kissed
for the first time in two years.

She looks again as she did at eighteen,
before the black hair and vinyl corsets.

I draw tarot cards in her secret room,
my boyfriend in pleasant dreams downstairs.

My blood runs even with my breath and I
Am my teenage self again.

I know she is lonely, even without the cards.
It doesn't help I'm so far away.

In the night on the borrowed bed,
my boyfriend tells me distraction stories.

I can't say I listened. I could hear her voice
upstairs, gentle murmurs over railings.

And suddenly I'm leaving. We're on the train
out of Toronto. I'm staring at my dirty sneakers.

She is sad.

I'm afraid I'll lose her.

Sodas and ice cream in the Union Station.
We wait for the train.

When my boyfriend wanders off, I confess,
Mina, I hate to go.

I want to roam Toronto like we did at nineteen, wallow
in the dirty grime of Queen Street,

ramshackle basements and barely functioning bathrooms,
industrial goth clubs with papier-mâché gargoyles.

She is gentle when she reveals.

Our teenage friends are gone.
The clubs have gone prep.

Queen Street is a joke and we're older now.
We want meaning, not innocence.

She's right.

But the grip on my throat stays when I leave,
and she is left behind again to swirl in my memories,

both past and present as the train moves away.

She is my split personality, my baby Aphrodite
from Aldershot to Aberdeen

I watch over her as best as I can,
but she is split, after all.

Barcelona

I met a girl with red dreadlocks
and Robin Hood eyes.

I never would have guessed
she was Spanish from her pale freckles.

Her accent reminded me of Las Ramblas,
La Sagrada Familia.

Unstuck my frozen memories of
fragrance peace, war protests,

battered bed sheets over balconies
and 'American-style' donuts

served without judgment. The happy ache
left behind in Gerona.

She makes photocopies. I stalk a map
desperate to pinpoint where I once

walked, slept, spoke the language.
God, I want to impress her.

But I'm caught behind a desk in America
And too quickly, she is gone.

Distance Over Time

I know these routes so well.
Four, five times a year,

I venture through the same old fields,
pale, cold rivers.

I've never stopped to say hello.
Seems I've spent

a quarter life
in these metal tubes

with chilly air,
coat backdrop

two seats to myself,
sleeping away hours at a time.

Overseas Flight

By the look of the horizon,
we're flying into cool fire.

As night comes, the skylines
change, color to shade

azure blue to cream.
No one else is even looking.

They're all slumped over,
asleep in their seats.

A dream wave must have washed over,
and forgotten about me.

Their loss. The clouds are winking
as the stars play tag in the distance.

To Walk Afraid

Tree trunks burst
in a joyful explosion.
A maple dips another
in a dance as
the bush children watch.

Oak seems to bow
and extend its leafy palm.
Squirrels play tag,
wind around a hickory
like a bark tree carousel,
like gray ribbons around a pole.

Inside their canopies
I am enthralled, but scared.
Too many green shadows
and mysterious twigs.
I'm alone on this path.
No one to scream for.
My mind puts up her fists.

Inside, I know nothing
will happen, but a girl's
fear is learned early.
Anything tall carries
a kind of threat.

I sit on a bridge of jagged,
mismatched redwood. My legs dangle.
The water dribbles in rock rivers
over twig dams. I think of crawfish
and nipped toes that leak
drops of cloudy red.

I pull my feet away.
A chicken.
A scaredy-cat
changed
by the daily news.

Paul Morgan

Londoner's Love Song

In keeping with the habit of the Age
I will not get to know you well.
Time is too short, so much to do.
We will talk often by mobile
or even mouth should chance
bring us rarely together.
I will send you emails
apologising for not ringing.
Our diaries will clash on our behalf.
In truth, sometimes,
I wonder why we married.

Flying Lesson

Unaided I could fly, swooping and diving.
No Icarus was I for what was there about me
that could melt? – no wings necessary;
just the will not to be on my feet and
no ambition for cloud lands that only freeze.
I knew the secret and could tell it, so soon
it was a family affair. We had a journey to make
to a place and for a purpose I cannot now recall
if indeed I ever knew.
Low we went and fast, laughing at the surprise
on every ground-fast face. We swerved between them
just inches from the pavement. At first we flew sitting
as if on invisible seats: our magic was prosaic,
but soon we became bolder.
Once I broke away down a peeling corridor to a dingy bar and
through it without stopping to order: no greater intoxication needed.
After the swerves came now the swoops, clearing buildings with
outspread limbs and unpractised ease, for confidence and skill
came without effort. I tell you there was no fear and why should you
disbelieve this plain fact? (Pilate asked what truth was, but I know
he never flew – except in old jokes)
I let the others go on and perched on a chimney pot to think this
out. How did I know old Pontius never flew?
One night in Judea he could have dreamed of soaring over the sea
to Rome. But I dismissed that at once as irrelevant, for I was not
dreaming.
For me then, on that hard unsteady roost, I was in the real world
that had brought me sudden and unlooked for grace, just as true as
all the griefs and joys that buffet and bend us from our first
breathing.
I knew I had the knowledge of the birds, but no need of wings or
mighty muscles. All I had to do was clear and simple – to be
freely shared as soon as I was ready. But that was for later: now my
companions were gone and I was just sitting. It was time to fly
again.

Time to fly again, but now without remembrance of how I had first begun. The chimney pot was suddenly steeple high. A time for thought to cease. I trusted and toppled forward. A slither on damp slates and then, and then, a joyful soar.

And I knew the secret again and I knew that trust was part of it. Not all of it, but the soul of it, if a secret can have a soul. So much easier to trust when flying. Staying low now, arms out-flung, along a road straight and deep between hushed trees. It was growing dark, but I did not doubt I would find the others.

I was with them again and we flew together among high silent ruins of factories. All life was gone from their gaunt bricks and chimneys but we were not oppressed, so full were we of our common gift. For us they were not lifeless husks of expectation: they were a playground in which we wheeled and circled.

Then I woke up quite suddenly. For a moment I thought I still had the secret, but the shade of Pilate sniggered as I walked to catch my train.

All that in me Weeps

All that in me weeps in old regret
for a child long sleeping,
who ran on a green hillside
and guessed the stories of the clouds.
Who played when roads were hot,
the sweet tar smell enfolding laughter
in the summer sun
that can no longer warm me.
When milk was cold and clean
in the new morning
and all things were bright and beautiful
in the steep grey streets.
All that in me knows there's no return
to that ancient keeping.

Xerxes

Xerxes was a Persian king
who hated Greeks like anything.
It wasn't that they were so bad;
It's just that they had stuffed his dad
at Marathon, (you know the place,
it gave its name to that long race).
The great king rather liked to win
by killing people fat or thin
and strewing them all over town
and burning lots of buildings down.
He liked girls and he liked treasure
but he preferred this darker pleasure.
So off he marched with his big army
and no one dared to call him barmy,
for if he heard what they had said
he soon relieved them of their head.
He built a great big bridge of boats
"Oh jolly good," he said, "it floats."
Then keeping up a fearful pace,
he marched his brave lads into Thrace.
Unhappily for Xerxes' plot
Themistocles had heard the lot.
When he did, he cried "Good gravy!
Here's a nice job for our navy."
On land as well he had a plan.
The Spartan king, the very man,
to head them off up at the pass
(his name it was Leonidas).
The pass was called Thermopylae,
and Leo got there after tea,
just in time to stop the Persians,
says history in all its versions.

Although he ended up quite dead,
Leonidas, the Greeks all said,
would be remembered as a hero,
rather than a living zero.
Before Xerxes could take the piss
he lost at sea at Salamis.
He gnashed his teeth; he tore his wig:
He'd lost and really lost quite big
"You, Greeks," he wailed, "I hate and curse ya!"
and buggered off right back to Persia.

Called to Account

How will you tally your days?
In the slow dusk of age,
or life's sudden spilling
you will have time,
an instant of eternity,
for remembrance and regret.
Times forgotten and unwelcome recalling;
ancient leaves stir in the wind
and crumble in your hand.
Fears come to pass and unfulfilled,
fading hopes and melting dreams.
First distant brightness,
when nothing was revealed,
flickers and dims.
And in that final silence,
as life takes its leave,
how will you tally your days?

Not dead but sleeping

I was not dead, but sleeping
when you went and buried me.
Can you not now hear me calling
from the old town cemetery?
My grave is cold and lonely.
I wish that I could leave;
even for just one day only,
to see whether you grieve.
For I have a strong suspicion,
you were glad to see me go;
glad to send me to perdition,
glad to pick up all my dough.
(This box is quite constricting:
I can't move an arm or leg,
and the screwed down lid's restricting
the very breath with which I beg.)
So I guess there's not much longer
for me in darkness here to lie.
I'm not getting any stronger,
will never know the reason why.
Why you stuck the kitchen cleaver
in so deep between my ribs,
and became a story weaver;
told the coppers all those fibs.
Just a moment, now I can gauge
Why no one can hear me call:
since you sliced right through my rib cage
I am stone dead after all.
Well blimey there's a thought,
so I'm really just a stiff.
No point getting overwrought
about our lethal lovers' tiff.
'Cos I don't just have to lie here
in this cold and lonely grave
I can haunt you now my dear.
I hope you're feeling brave.

Old Man's Mirror

Mirror and photograph:
neither can lie but one does
as time shrivels former truth.
A lifetime ago I laughed at old fools
that I have trailed each short day.
Robbed of a child's wisdom,
I have replaced it with certainties,
born of nameless errors
and have ignored the withering years.
Until reflection's crooked smile
and cracked brow beckoned
me to sleep.

Do not Mourn the Flying Suns

Do not mourn the flying suns.
Let them flicker in mind's eye
and then forget them.
It cannot be that night will never come,
that you'll not join the shades
and be forgotten.
Consider it a loosing of chains
and an early leaving of labour.
Go into the dark without regret.

Gethsemane

I did not ask you to go to the Garden and so
I do not see why I should blame myself
for what happened then or later befell you.
You were a grown man, kneeling in a trap
of your own free making.

The decisions, founded in your love of Love itself,
that took you to that garden,
and those of hate filled Hitler
to feed the Auschwitz ovens
with so many distant children
of those who chose to kill you,
through their ignorance or fear,
are each not of my making nor of anyone alive.

Words and deeds show you both sensible and politic,
rendering unto Caesar and also unto God,
avoiding lawyers' snares with polished ease.
And yet, and yet.
At time of high emotion
you rode in public clamour
through the gateway of your enemies,
past sentries of the occupying power.
This seems to me unwise in the extreme.

At Passover! With Jews recalling rescue
from ancient oppression,
under the nervous noses of their new oppressors,
you came and were acclaimed as the Messiah:
a threat to spearmen and scribes alike.

Then you vandalised the Temple stalls,
disturbing lawful business,
ensuring men of power would seek
your speedy liquidation.
How clearly can I see
you came in search of death.

When you knelt in lonely vigil in the garden of Gethsemane
you knew full well the end was very near.
A long and dusty road behind, a ghastly cup ahead.

Had you seen a crucifixion
in the course of your long wanderings?
If so, no wonder you sought
a gentler path to peace.
You were a man in torment,
lonely under the stars,
when you made your final choosing
and the men with torches came.

You left the garden pinioned,
followers fleeing in the dark.
No more decisions to make,
only the familiar formalities
of show trial and judicial murder.
A dangerous revolutionary killed
to keep peace for and between Romans and Jews.
A story ended in agonised asphyxiation.

So this is where my logic leads.
A man died but I did not kill him.

How is it then times come
when I know without doubting
that I too stand mocking by the Cross,
happy that another and not I
hangs torn and pierced and bleeding
under sullen sky.

Rite of Passage

When you smack
you say
it hurts you more
than it hurts me.
I'm sure you're wrong.
You don't cry
and rub your hand
like I do my leg.
Also you are
bigger, much bigger
than me.
It must hurt me more.
One day when I am
bigger, much bigger
than you.
I'll smack you and see.
Like Daddy does,
when you are naughty.

Tony Lewis-Jones

Talking Blues

Tonight we are listening to the Blues
because at this point there is nothing else to say.
The Delta rhythms tell of harsh wrongs
and oppression; some guy with an unlikely name
conjures old magic from the night, and soon
the wine bottle between us will be drained.

I have never learned guitar, and your sweet
singing voice has been neglected, but we are
true to the spirit of these lamentations:
our silence speaks beneath the fading song.
I want to hear that minstrel howling at the moon.
I pass the bottle, start the tape again.

This Year

This year, I gave her a blood-red rose.
Heaven knows, there's been enough blood spilled
and the need for peace is greater than ever.

I hope she'll keep it till it's dry, and then
place it between the covers of a book she loves,
and find it later, with surprise and pleasure.

What more can we do in these unquiet times?
Too much blood-red grief has fallen
on the world to be assuaged by flowers.

Off the Record

These unguarded moments
which are never made public
between people–the long tears
she shed after her mother's funeral:
an angel counted them all,
has numbered them.

This early morning, getting dressed
she snagged a nail on her tights, and laughed
and cursed, and I thought how privileged
I am to know her when the masks
are down. Our lives are full

of secrets which might mean
nothing to anybody else, which only
ourselves and the wise angels ever see.

Late Flowers

We are travelling the edges of discovery.
Your nearness frightens sometimes.
This years-long ache has grown
a further decibel, and we're between
restraint and yearning for what might arise.

Summer has a few warm nights left in her.
Late flowers line your straight road
to the coast. The radio is playing
another ballad about leaving. Needing you,
wanting you. Love songs, pretty lies.

The Lesser Light

The moon has seen it all before in dreams:
the lovers' kiss, the midnight masquerade,
the child squalling in a humble cradle.
Remembers too, though distant, time's revenges
which, like the turning tides, leave on the shore
the husks of meaning that composed our lives
as so much flotsam for scavengers to pick.

The knowing moon shines on, and will outlast
small stars in earthly galaxies, and if
her presence is a pale foretelling of the sun
she has seen half our history, and often
our darker purposes. The betrayer
took the bread, although his heart had turned,
then took himself outside. And it was night.

The Dead will Rise

Maybe a sense of history is not important.
After all, the winners write the books,
the official version is handed down, received
and passed from generation to generation.

I would like to hear what the losers think,
the ones who lost their families, their homes,
and had their country taken over.
Or from the shade of the soldier I saw dead

(I do not know or care his nationality)
on the front page of the paper. Tell me, friend,
was any of it worth your life? You have a story,
and tonight, it's quiet. Let me hear you speak.

Amsterdam Oktober

There is always a price to be paid
in Amsterdam. From the beggars
who know the value of everything
to the British couple, sitting on the large
floating hotel, watching the river pass.
We have the look of satisfied lovers.
And others, who bustle by their Friday nights
are Lost In Music and the ceaseless flow.

Tomorrow will be a day for packing.
We raided shops for Christmas things, the light
of the clearing sky reflecting on
this city that is built on water and
people having fun. Or not. And is that why
the woman in purple at the Silver Store paused
over the crucifix you wanted for your sister?
'You came prepared,' her mute smile seemed to say.

An End to Waiting

I have learned patience from the lives of saints
who kept their holiness through misery
mindful always of the light that shines.

But now you're here, and, without restraint,
we answer to the flesh obediently.
The saints have their reward, and I have mine.

While She is Away

The moon can't settle to its work. Our cats,
who know a thing or two about
the cyclical nature of existence,
wander in and out of the kitchen, follow
scents of other animals in the flower-beds.

There is a stillness that does not feel right. It feels
like imminence, like the words we should have
said last night, or not at all, and which
remain unsaid between us. This
emptiness she always leaves behind her

is all-consuming. While she is away
the minutes crumble and the hours decay.

Voices Off

Often, when the thunder rolls to heaven
and people hide from the rain
and the lightning descends faster than
an eye blinking, it reminds me forcibly
of war, and the war-like: the all-powerful Generals
issuing orders that must end in death
for the off-spring of lovers on both sides of the wire,

And I wonder how I would fare with a gun:
whether the blood of my fathers would tell me,
by instinct, the way to behave and what has to be done.

Enough. She is beside me, sleeping,
and we are in love. There will be
time for war when the time is given.
In the darkness, my consciousness drifts like a ghost
through the noise of the thunder in which
even prayers are lost.

Biographies

Andrew Proudfoot was born in Hertfordshire, in the UK, in 1962. A voracious reader of Science Fiction and Fantasy from the age of twelve, Andrew's first attempts at writing were in a similar vein. He was first drawn to poetry in his late teens – initially inspired by the work of Robert Lowell and John Betjeman and later by Roger McGough (all of whom remain favourites to this day), although it wasn't until 1994 that he first penned his own verse. There followed a barren eight-year period before he discovered an internet writing group in 2002 and resumed poetry writing. Andrew is motivated by the everyday and the mundane, and is "absolutely terrified of the empty page and of the responsibility which goes with it". A Civil Servant working in IT, Andrew currently lives in Plymouth with his wife, a teenage daughter and four cats.

Jan Oskar Hansen is a Norwegian poet who lives in Portugal and borrows the English language when writing poetry. Jan is a former cook in the merchant navy and first began writing poetry in Norwegian, but was met with contempt by Oslo editors. Jan switched to using the English language and his poems have since been published worldwide. *Letters from Portugal* (BeWrite Books, 2003) is Jan's first collection of poetry.

John Thomson, born in the 1960's, lives in Kilsyth, near Glasgow, Scotland. Married with two grown sons, John has been writing seriously since the late 1990's. He has been published in many small press magazines, including *Acorn*, *Carillon* and *Aesthetica*. His biggest influences include T.S. Eliot, Dylan Thomas and Philip Larkin, and interests include reading, writing and football (soccer to anyone outside the UK).

Clive Warner used to travel the world installing radio stations, usually in places where no tourist would want to set foot. When broadcast satellites arrived his career disappeared. Eventually he emigrated from England to Mexico, where he now lives with his wife, two children, Rocky the cantankerous retriever, Timmy the cat, and Shelley the desert tortoise. Clive's first published novel, an action-adventure, *Appointment in Samara* was published in June 2002. He writes poetry as well as fiction, and loves to take part in readings, slams, and any literary event, simply because 'writers are such great people!'

Kathryn McL. Collins is a native New Yorker now living in New Jersey, whose works have been described as "a gentle sort of poetry", "those of a poet's poet". Instilled at an early age with a love of poetry by her dear grandmother, Kitty, who quoted Longfellow by rote, Kathy expresses a humble gratitude for simply being. The sudden death in 1995 of her daughter, Jeanne, age 21, has greatly influenced Kathy's poetry and enriched her appreciation of loving relationships. In fact, it was after Jeannie's death poetry emerged. Each poem is an expression of deep and abiding love for friends and family, who support and inspire, most especially her husband, Neil and daughter, Colette. Kathy posts her work on several websites and regularly contributes to WritingForum.com, BeWrite.net, Riverwind Poetry and Windows of the Soul. Her work is featured in the anthology, *Across the Abyss*, published by The International Library of Poetry and *listening to the birth of crystals,* published by Paula Brown, proceeds to profit The National Deaf Children's Society and Merseyside Society for Deaf People, UK.

Darrel A Patterson was born in Pennsylvania, USA but became **Dazz Jackson** and relocated when the bill collectors heard about it. Bored after a couple of years' college in Atlanta, Georgia, he joined the US Army and learned about the world in places as far a field as Korea and Kuwait.

When the writing bug bit, Dazz, who's mid-thirties, mothballed the uniform and got to work. His fearful fascination with state-of-the-art military technology shows through in his work especially his short stories. Between the day job, baseball and football games on TV, cooking, his passions for interior design, ice-cold brews, his partner and his six year old son, Dazz has produced an impressive word portfolio, including an epic novel which is already in edit with BeWrite Books.

Tom O Campbell's photography and poetry have appeared in The Midday Moon, BeWrite.net, Head to Hand and Moon Reader. He recently relocated to the Midwest (United States) from Hollywood, California where he worked for producer Roger Corman on several movies including: Battle Beyond the Stars, Escape from New York, Forbidden World, Galaxy of Terror, Android, Space Raiders, Warlords from Hell, as well as various commercials and TV movies. He recently joined the board of community theatre Limelight Players in Belleville, Illinois and directed "Picasso at the Lapin Agile" for that company. He has worked as a test-driver, dairy manager, and riverboat captain. He has a degree in desktop publishing.

Born in Ottawa, Canada, **Heather Grace Stewart** wrote her first poem at five, inspired by falling down a lot while attempting to figure skate. *At the Arena* was published in her primary school's newsletter. From that moment, she was hooked on writing. At Queen's University in Kingston, Ontario, Heather honed her skills by writing poetry for the Queen's *Journal*, *ASH* literary journal and the *Tricolour* yearbook. After graduating in 1995 with a BA(H), she attended Concordia University in Montreal and received a graduate degree in Journalism. In 1999 she founded Graceful Publications, her freelance writing, editing, and photography agency.

BeWrite Books published her second book, *A Moment for Me*, a lined journal for busy adults that features thirty-one of her poems, in October 2002. She actually wrote some of the poems included in *Routes* in the lines inside her own copy of *A Moment for Me.* Heather was poetry editor at BeWrite.net long before they started their BeWrite Books line. She edited BeWrite's first-ever poetry anthology, *Shaken & Stirred* (2002), and recently edited Jan Oskar Hansen's first book of poems, *Letters from Portugal* (BeWrite Books, 2003). Heather is also the editor *Vinegar Moon*, Donna Biffar's first collection of poetry published by BeWrite Books. She lives in Québec with husband Bill, an engineer, and a couple of crazy cats (Sam and Shadow) that love to sit on her computer keyboard while she's trying to write. Visit her at: www.hgrace.com.

John G Hall was born in Manchester on the 4th of July 1959, the year of the Cuban Revolution, on American Independence Day. Revolt and irony were in his historical stars, though the same forces moved many of his generation growing up in the 1960's and 1970's. Although his father was an occasional artist, it was his mother who introduced John to the world of story-telling and storybooks. As he rattled on through the 1970's, his father suffered a massive stroke, which crippled him for life, and John's mother became nurse as well as a mother and a wife. His support through those times was the discovery of William Blake. In 1991 John left Manchester and became a student at Lancaster University studying Social History. Since his return to Manchester his poetry has taken centre stage. Since 2003 he's been increasingly published in print publications and on literary web sites throughout the world, including print publications such as *Fire*, *Carillion*, *The Ugly Tree*, *Rain Dog*, *Current Accounts*, *Running Water*, *The Wolf*, *Left Curve*, *Harlequin*, *Outlaw*, *Coffee House Poetry*, *Aesthetica*, *The Journal* and *The Peoples Poet Anthology II & III*. John is now organizing the publication of an arts and poetry magazine called *Citizen32*, themed on *War & Peace*, featuring such writers as Mario Petrucci, Jack Hirschman and Todd Swift.

Born and raised in Southern Ontario, Canada, **Heather Bryant** moved to Boston, Massachusetts at the age of twenty and currently resides in the New England region of the United States. She is the program director for the Rhode Island International Film Festival, poetry editor of BeWrite Books, and is currently involved in several writing projects as writer and editor.

Paul Morgan was born in Pontypridd, South Wales in 1954. He moved to North East England in 1980, got married and worked in industry as lawyer and commercial director for various bits of the Rolls-Royce group until 2000 when he became self-employed. He has written in a desultory fashion since childhood but quite a lot since the late 1990's including a novel, a radio play, a movie screenplay and a number of short stories as well as poems. 'All That in Me Weeps' was one of the first poems he ever wrote.

Tony Lewis-Jones was born in Wales, and educated at Clifton and New College, Oxford. His poetry has appeared in magazines and anthologies on both sides of the Atlantic, and in Australia, and has been broadcast on radio and TV. His sixth collection, *Full Moons And Half-Truths*, is now into its 4th edition. He has held and in some instances still holds a number of poetry-related posts, including Co-ordinator, Poetry In The Parks, Poet-In-Residence at BBC Radio Bristol and Poet-In-Residence at *The Bristol Evening Post*. He is married for the second time, and blessed with two fine children.

Index

Also Available from BeWrite Books

www.bewrite.net

Shaken and Stirred – Poetry from the Far Corners

'*Poetry does not belong in the mind. It belongs in the soul and in the bloodstream. Shaken and Stirred proves that brilliantly. This is a collection with great potential and one to which a reader of modern poetry will want to come back for inspiration, again and again.*'

Nicholas Cobic

Combine the poetic works of:

A Pennsylvania-born African-American who changed his name from Darrel to Dazz, left the army, and discovered that he had rhythm and rhyme.

The U.S.'s "Queen of the Small Presses": she's been called a "modern Emily Dickinson" and her work has been praised by Robert Frost.

A Norwegian-born poet who only started getting the attention he deserved once he started writing poems in his second language.

A senior lecturer in Political Science at Burdwan University, West Bengal, India, who writes about his love-hate relationship with Calcutta.

A busy mother of three from Adelaide, South Australia who found her muse at thirty-five.

Add the works of eight other talented poets – aiming for diversity in their backgrounds and writing styles – and mix in some revealing interviews.

ISBN 1-904224-85-7

A Moment for Me

by Heather Grace

A journal with poetry and photos by Canadian poet Heather Grace.

Perfect for busy adults who need to curl up and relax after a long day, this journal has plenty of space for lists, diary entries, short story plots, or poems of your own.

Decorated with poems about learning to relax, letting go, overcoming heartache, falling in love, parenting, even practising yoga on the beach and photos of serene moments in nature, this journal is the ideal gift for someone who seems to have everything.

Or why not pamper yourself for once? Pour some tea or coffee, and make a moment just for you.

ISBN 1-904224-96-2

Letters from Portugal

by Jan Oskar Hansen

"I never saw the beauty of the sea."

"My tree atop the hill murmurs its gratitude."

"Olive trees drip slow tears of immense sorrow, knowing they can never embrace one another."

Jan Oskar Hansen's attitudes are evident in his poetry: his wish that people were kinder and gentler; his abhorrence of war, his sense of humour about the senseless things people, including himself, have done.

But it's his love of plants, animals and all of nature – such a great admiration that he often uses personification, giving nature human qualities and emotions in his poems – that is most evident. Perhaps it's this quality – along with a tongue-in-cheek sense of humour – that makes his poems so unique and endearing.

Letters from Portugal is divided into six chapters: On Love, On War, On People, On Poetry, Hansen Snapshots, and Letters from Portugal: actual letters from the poet to his editor.

There's something for everyone here – even those who aren't frequent readers of poetry will be moved by Hansen's passion, amused by his sarcasm, and delighted by his ability to paint pictures of the simple things in ordinary life – making them extraordinary.

ISBN 1-904492-20-7

Crime	
The Knotted Cord	Alistair Kinnon
The Tangled Skein	Alistair Kinnon
Marks	Sam Smith
Porlock Counterpoint	Sam Smith
Scent of Crime	Linda Stone
Crime/Humour	
Sweet Molly Maguire	Terry Houston
Horror	
Chill	Terri Pine, Peter Lee, Andrew Müller
Fantasy/Humour	
Zolin A Rockin' Good Wizard	Barry Ireland
The Hundredfold Problem	John Grant
Earthdoom!	David Langford & John Grant
Fantasy	
The Far-Enough Window	John Grant
A Season of Strange Dreams	C. S. Thompson
Collections/ Short Stories	
The Loss of Innocence	Jay Mandal
Kaleidoscope	Various
Odie Dodie	Lad Moore
The Miller Moth	Mike Broemmel
Tailwind	Lad Moore
The Shadow Cast	Mike Broemmel
Humour	
The Cuckoos of Batch Magna	Peter Maughan
Thriller	
Deep Ice	Karl Kofoed
Blood Money	Azam Gill
Evil Angel	RD Larson
Disremembering Eddie	Anne Morgellyn
Flight to Pakistan	Azam Gill
Matabele Gold	Michael J Hunt
Removing Edith Mary	Anne Morgellyn
Historical Fiction	
Ring of Stone	Hugh McCracken

Jahred and The Magi	Wilma Clark

Contemporary

The Care Vortex	Sam Smith
Someplace Like Home	Terrence Moore
Sick Ape	Sam Smith
A Tangle of Roots	David Hough

Young Adult

Rules of the Hunt	Hugh McCracken
The Time Drum	Hugh McCracken
Kitchen Sink Concert	Ishbel Moore
The Fat Moon Dance	Elizabeth Taylor
Grandfather and The Ghost	Hugh McCracken
Return from the Hunt	Hugh McCracken

Children's

The Secret Portal	Reno Charlton
The Vampire Returns	Reno Charlton

Autobiography/Biography

A Stranger and Afraid	Arthur Allwright
Vera & Eddy's War	Sam Smith

General

The Wounded Stone	Terry Houston
Magpies and Sunsets	Neil Alexander Marr
Redemption of Quapaw Mountain	Bertha Sutliff

Romance

A Different Kind of Love	Jay Mandal
The Dandelion Clock	Jay Mandal

Coming Soon

As the Crow Flies	Dave Hutchinson
Masters of the Hunt	Hugh McCracken
Gemini Turns	Anne Marie Duquette
The Kinnons of Candleriggs	Jenny Telfer Chaplin

Printed in the United States
20772LVS00001B/171

9 781904 492603